A TOUR DE FRANCE

Paul Frederick Weston

Foreword by Suzanne Mullen

A Tour de France

by Paul Frederick Weston

Foreword by Suzanne Mullen

First Published in Great Britain in 2024 by Beercott Books, Kineton, Warwickshire, United Kingdom.

Text © Paul Frederick Weston 2020 & Suzanne Mullen 2024

Cover illustrations © Simon Lucas 2024

Design & layout © Beercott Books 2024

ISBN 978-1-7393020-7-8

Beercott

Contents

Foreword

In life, "they" (whoever "they" are?) say that all people have a book in them, a story which should be told. My dad had so many. He told lots of stories and had lots of stories to tell, through his childhood, then working within the Birmingham City Police Force, then West Midlands Police, of which he was very proud to be a member, then into his retirement years. He was also amazing at making stories up too, many times as children John and I, then his grandchildren, Adam, Lucy, Calum, and Daniel, would go to bed tucked up with dad/grandad asking for a subject that the story was going to be about, so whether it was giants, or teddy bears, aliens or monsters, my dad told the most amazing bedtime stories too. So, as I said, "they" say that all people have a book in them, here's just one of those stories which on this occasion happens to be true, not made up, which stars my dad. It was a dream he had had for a long time, then he made it a reality, not sure it initially stood up to the dream, but it got there.

Love you, Dad.
Suzanne x

Introduction

This is a story of a Policeman who, on retirement, decided to travel through France on a bicycle. There is nothing special about it, no dramatic incidents happened, it's just a record of what went on before he forgets. "The Fat Man on a Bike" has already been done, but you only saw him pedalling on flat bits. This is me, warts and all, as known to my family, friends, and perhaps one day, my grandchildren. I'd like to dedicate it to my family, who have put up with me and the police, and with all the restrictions that has meant for them. To Jackie for being the best wife possible, and to Suzanne and John, for growing up into people I'm proud to say are my children.

Paul Weston (September 1944 - August 2020)

A "TOUR DE FRANCE"
Part 1

Chapter One

I should state immediately, should any analyst of the Police mind ever read this story, that I write it, not to cleanse myself from the pain and anguish of thirty and half years of service, because I had a wonderful time as a copper, but simply because I had a terrible time on my personal miniadventure. I'd like others to laugh with me, or at me, because, on reflection, I really enjoyed it. If you have a dream, go for it, I did, and I recommend you do the same. Life's too short to leave things 'till tomorrow.

However, to appreciate why I chose to abuse my body in France, you do need to have the background, and as stated, it is rooted in a lifetime of Police Service. Thirty plus years in any job is a long time, so as my retirement date from the service drew near, I decided that unlike many other officers, who bought new cars, boats etc, using part of their pension fund, I would travel through France for several weeks.

Not original! but I might return a rested and possibly even a healthier man, and if fate took a hand, and the wine and foie gras overcame me, then I was still heavily insured.

You might also notice that my trip was going to cost a lot

less than any car, but I assure you that I am no skinflint.

The first task was to prepare the ground for the great adventure, which I intended to make on my own. I had already passed the word at work that my trip was in the planning stage, so that the traditional retirement collection, plus the 30-year monetary award the Force provides, (about £105), could be used to buy something appropriate for the holiday.

I had provisionally checked a sailing from Poole in Dorset, which would deposit me at Cherbourg, 20 to 25 miles from the town of Bricquebec-en-Cotentin which I wanted to revisit. In anticipation of major problems in persuading my wife, I began to drop little hints that this was what I wanted to do for my retirement present.

I'd mentioned it years earlier, so my wife knew the thought was in my mind, but formal permission had not yet been granted. What fools we men are! There I was, thinking I was persuading her, when all the time, armed with information from my daughter, my full intentions were known, my plans were in the enemy's hands, and the result of the battle had been decided.

I just wanted to wander through France! and hand on heart, I had no ulterior motives. Going to France on your own for rest and recuperation, obviously means different things to a husband than to a wife. My intentions were honourable, and it was at this early stage of the trip that my wife made certain that they stayed that way. Looking back, I am equally certain that her suggestions as to transport were a double bluff, intended to ensure that I refused her advice, thereby forcing me to select the pedal bike as a means of travel, and ultimately causing the failure of the expedition. (That's my story anyway).

"I was not then, am not now, and never have been", a

handsome man. I may have been reasonable when I was young, but at 49 yrs. and 9 months, the years had taken their toll, and I could definitely say I was not handsome. To prove my point, I stood about six feet one inch tall and weighed in then at about 22 stone. Much of this excess baggage was, and still is, carried at the front and rear, so it is a great compliment to my wife's affection for me, that she might have seen me, even marginally, in the role of Don Juan, though it was France I was visiting, not Spain.

My plan was to take 6 weeks travelling through France, stopping at farms as I went. I meant to introduce myself to the occupiers, and in exchange for the use of a field as a place to pitch my tent, offered to help with small tasks the following day. Not only would my French improve, but I would really get a feeling for the true taste of French life. If afterwards, retirement proved too boring, my better grasp of the language might provide me with a new job in the European Community. I had selected my mode of transport so that I would return, a lean, mean, fighting machine.

This is where the sheer cunning of the female mind always defeats the male, for without any argument, she agreed that I could go! All my reasons carefully developed last thing at night as I was dozing off, so much wasted effort. All my "But Darlings" practised with just the right pleading tone, useless. Then, when I was totally dumbstruck at this easy capitulation, the masterstroke! She suggested that the bike would "probably be a little bit too much for me", and that I should "take the car", but "strap the bike on the back to potter around" when I "got to places". What male ego could stand for such an insult! Take the car! rubbish! potter around? Never! I would cycle around France with a tent and minimum equipment, to return triumphant, six weeks later! I would be bronzed by the sun and wind, muscles where muscles had long since disappeared, proving her wrong in every department.

Isn't it galling when your wife knows you so well? By that simple ploy, she had sowed the seeds of failure and if there was any lingering doubt as to my behaviour when away, she had ensured nothing could possibly happen! You see, if I had taken the car, then sitting in it, and paraphrasing Gilbert and Sullivan, "I might have looked alright in the dark with the light behind me" but what self-respecting French woman would look twice at 22 stone of buttocks drooping over a saddle at the rear, while a belly was supported on a pair of handlebars at the front of a bicycle, which had most definitely, like the rider, seen better days.

I could have done it, you know! It was her! Having already made certain that male pride would make me go on the bike, she made her second move and suggested that "If I was intent on going, then surely the bike ought to have a strengthened frame, to cope with my size".

Another low blow! Calculated to make me decline her offer, and take an old machine, (I had already decided on a sensible style), even further reducing my chances of success. There was nothing wrong with an old, but refurbished, sit up and beg Raleigh, in the Police style, with a big, soft, saddle. It would be more than sufficient. "A little bit of exercise perhaps before you go? just to tone you up dear" she said. Rubbish! The idea was to get fit on the trip, there was little point in getting fit beforehand, or indeed doing exercise before I started. Didn't she understand? I now believe she did, only too well.

There was a cycle repair shop attached to the school for the visually impaired in Harborne, Birmingham. I was certain that they would have the sort of bike I was looking for or would know where I could get one. Some of you may see a slight problem in buying a bicycle which has been put together by a partially sighted person, but you would be wrong! The bike had been completely renovated and looked brand new. There was only one   part of it which gave me trouble throughout the trip, but the people at the school would have needed to have cycled to have tested it. More will be revealed later..........

The fact was, I was wrong, I should have taken the car!

With the purchase of a few elastic ropes, some tyre levers, spare brake blocks, inner tube, chain links, and a pair of panniers, I was almost ready. All that remained was shelter. This was supplied, in the form of a two-man igloo tent, together with some other delightful retirement presents by my colleagues at work. I responded by inviting about seventy of them to a local Curry House, at my expense. There my erstwhile Boss (whose nickname I can now reveal was The Rottweiler), said nice things about me all of which were true, while I replied by saying nasty things about him now that I had retired, all of which   were probably true and provided amusement to the rest of the guests.

Sacrifices were necessary! There was insufficient space to take either sleeping bag or bed roll in my opinion. In any case, where I was going it didn't rain, and the nights were warm. Not only that, but I was sure I would be so tired after cycling all day, that I would sleep soundly even on hard ground. Anyway, I might be offered a bed by my hosts.

The nights were cold! No-one offered me a bed! But I did get two things right. The ground was hard and at least on the first night I was so shattered I could have slept on the crossbar.

The day of my departure was approaching, and as a last

preparation, I had a letter drawn up by a good friend and colleague Ron Pearce, who spoke fluent French and German, so that should I have a problem, I could produce it to the local police (I totally forgot this when I needed it). Another friend and workmate, Geoff Young, bought me a traveller's guide to France which was and still is used every time I go there, and I bought maps of my projected route, and booked the ferry. First impressions are important, and I wanted the French to see me at my best, so rather than tire myself cycling to Poole, I bought a train ticket for myself and the bike at Birmingham New Street, having of course saved further effort by bringing the bike home from Harborne in a trailer, borrowed from "Uncle" Bill.

The day arrived! Even having cut down on luxuries, the bike seemed well stocked, so it seemed sensible to husband my resources. A phone call later, Uncle Bill supplied the trailer again, and off to the station we went, the bike and load bouncing around behind us. It's clear to me now, that in some strange way, the bike preferred to be carried, rather than do the carrying (see later).

I was wearing a pair of jogging style trousers of a woolly material, a similar style top, green coloured trainers, (which I soon found made your feet stink to high heaven) and a rather natty white hat. I had a sort of leather purse come body belt, which you wore like a shoulder holster. This was not because I wanted to look macho, but it was the most convenient way to carry your papers and cash when cycling, rather than have them fall out of a back pocket. I was confident that the clothing and associated colour scheme befitted an English ambassador to the French. A photo, just before loading, shows that I did indeed look a picture!

I must here record how touched I was by my family's concern as they saw me off. The tears were genuine. Would I be safe? They were racked with sobs, hidden behind hands held close to their distorted faces. If it had been anyone else, I might have thought it was hysterical laughter, rather than tears.

I was delivered, complete with the bike in the trailer, about a hundred yards from the station and nonchalantly taking the handlebars, pushed it onto the concourse. It was really heavy and unwieldy. Was this an omen? I refused to be worried by these negative thoughts. I had seen the roads of La Belle France when driving the car. They seemed to be dead flat for miles and miles. Once on them, time would speed along, my body would harden and trim down, I would be tanned and fit, while at night I would lie beneath the stars, a bottle of wine in one hand, a lump of cheese and a baguette in the other.

I couldn't get the bike down the stairs onto the platform at the station! No doubt about it, it was heavy, and the panniers kept falling to one side. A porter tried to help me carry it down, which in itself was unusual, but gave up and let me use the goods lift instead. I rested the thing up against a bench seat and sat down to wait for the train.

We English are a strange nation! Can you believe that with all those people waiting like me, not one even said hello. Lots of them seemed to be examining both me and the bike whilst smiling or was it laughing? I could see little to smile about, but in my old job I was used to strange looks. Besides, I was more concerned by how much the push from my drop off point to the station, and the struggle into the lift had tired me. It was going to be good to be fit again.

When the train arrived, the guard helped me to lift the thing into the van, where I chained it to the steel mesh cage so

11

that it wouldn't be stolen. Looking back, that would have been a wonderful excuse to have gone straight home. I doubt that anyone would have been desperate enough to steal it. I remember thinking that the guard must have suffered from bad breath or had a cold coming on. He kept covering his mouth with his hand, and alternately holding his stomach while making muffled choking noises. I wondered if he had suffered a hernia while man-handling the bike? Whatever it was, it only developed after I had told him what I was going to do, and he recovered quickly, as he was all smiles as he waved his green flag. It was good to see someone enjoying his job.

We pulled away, and the excitement of the start of my trip came to me. I can remember thinking how great it was going to be. The 6th of June 1994, D-day's 50th anniversary, had been my retirement day from the Force, but now, on the 27th I felt as if my retirement had really started. This trip marked a new point in my life, no matter what the outcome.

Chapter Two

I was booked on the night sailing on Truckline ferries, and it was about 8pm when we arrived at Poole. The journey down had been uneventful. Just as in the station no one spoke to me. Looking as I did, and wearing what looked like a shoulder holster, I can understand. I dozed, I might even have slept, I am skilled in both disciplines, and finally, we stopped at Bournemouth, disgorged some passengers, then edged along the line the few miles to Poole. This was it. I could put it off no longer! The time had come to mount the machine. Into the van I went. The guard had duties elsewhere or I am sure he would have helped, so I struggled on my own, and after unlocking the bike, manoeuvred it to the doors, and putting my shoulder under the crossbar lifted it down onto the platform.

There was a little sloping road from the platform onto the car park which gave me some momentum. It was getting dark, so I dropped the dynamo onto the tyre and rode off into the night. Sounds almost romantic, doesn't it? The power being generated by my speed was minimal, and so naturally, the lights were equally dim. I reminded myself to ensure I only travelled by day in France. I didn't want to be run down on the right-hand side of the road. I suppose I should have had a little refresher at cycling before doing it in the dark surrounded by lorry drivers going to the ferry. Truth to tell, I would probably have been safer riding on the right in France, since half the lorries which kept buffeting me with their passing seemed to be British. There was a major problem of lack of ability after thirty years of driving. I hadn't exactly forgotten how to ride but visualise this. Heavily laden, unbalanced, unknown streets, looking for the signs with little ships on them, in the dark, on a bike which had yet to acknowledge its master. Add the bumpy, uneven, and cobbly streets around that harbour area, and it was a miracle I ever got to the ferry. Even this early in my trip, the "Romance" of bike riding was already being transmitted to my rear end. I began to reconsider! I remembered the phrase I had learnt when in training at Harrogate, "Failing to plan is planning to fail", and realised that it might have more relevance to me and my bike trip, than to a 50-minute lesson on "Lights on Pedal Cycles Regulations".

If you ever visit Poole, then as you pass over the swing bridge between the inner and outer harbours, you come to a little traffic island. You can turn left towards the ferries, or like me, if you have a little time to spare before boarding, you can turn right, and stop at the chippy about 200 yards along the road on the left. Come on! I'd only had a snack on the train! my bum was hurting; I had cycled about half a mile! And it was going to be 6 weeks before I tasted the culinary delights of England again. Since I was going to lose all that weight anyway, I felt I deserved a last treat. A beautiful piece of cod and chips in one hand and a recalcitrant bike in the other, I wobbled along the road back towards the ferries and Poole harbour. As I left the shop, I felt proud to be British. The chippy and his assistant had wanted to know what I was doing, and I had laid out my plans to them. It was touching. They both came outside to wave me off. They tried to hide it, but I saw, as I tried to re-find my biking skills, that, hands to their faces, they were crying with emotion. I had obviously impressed them.

Regular users of the Poole route to the Continent, will know that at 9pm at night there are no queues to board the ferries. This night was no exception. The traffic lanes, and there are 20 or 30 of them, were almost empty, and in any case, the man at the front who tells you where to go, seeing my glimmering front light, and a large man apparently floating above it, waved me down to the head of the lane. I arrived to see him looking nonplussed.

He looked at me as though he was wondering where my car was? as if any minute, my wife, and children would appear with a heavily loaded vehicle. Was I merely keeping their place for them? When, after a few minutes no one else arrived to accompany me, and it became clear that I was alone, save for my faithful steed, he took one half of my ticket, gave me the other half, and walked off muttering into his radio something about a Tanker?

Have you ever noticed how awkward bikes are when there isn't anywhere to lean them? I have, and most of that thinking was done between 9pm and 10pm on the night I left England. You can either stand astride the crossbar, which then has a tendency to keep falling to one side or the other and bruising, (for the want of delicacy), one's inner thighs. Or you may lean the bike towards yourself at an angle, and in turn lean back against the crossbar, which bruises an equally soft part of one's anatomy. So, an hour passed, my bike and I had been gazed on by truckers, car drivers, children, motor cyclists, pedestrians, lorries full of cows, sheep, and pigs, but another cyclist? nary a one. I was it! The sole representative of English cycling using that particular ferry that night.

Engines revved, smoke belched, and the huge lorries were the first to be marshalled towards the ferry, driving into the lower deck. It took a few seconds to realise that the "Oi's" and "Hey you's" were directed at me, but ignoring the shouting and with growing ability, I casually pedalled towards the boat. There was a slight incline as I reached the ramps, so I dismounted, nonchalantly throwing my leg over the crossbar (the old skills were returning), and keeping well to the right, avoiding the holes, tie bars, chains and things welded into the deck, I pushed my machine into the lorry level.

A French seaman was at the sharp end of the boat, about 300 yards away shouting unintelligible things about "Camions, Les Anglais" and "Idiots sur velos" so, intent on displaying what we English were made of, I remounted and cycled towards him, avoiding the aforesaid, bits and pieces on the deck. It was during this relatively small ride, that I learnt the best method of decapitation next to the guillotine, and the first rule of cycling. That being, that "a lorry driver's door is set at just the right height when swung open unexpectedly, to remove a cyclist's head, no matter what the nationality of the lorry." While disconcerting, it was a useful lesson learnt on a ship, before venturing onto the roads, and I grudgingly thanked the driver of a "Norbert Dentressangle" pantechnicon for my education and proving that my reactions were still quite sharp.

I was now approaching the aforesaid seaman at the sharp end, and since I thought I could speak French reasonably, I was looking forward to my first opportunity of extending my knowledge of the language with this son of the sea. His French accent was a mixture of a garlic laden belch, combined with a dash of Dorset, but the eloquence of the large dirty thumb, with which he gestured to a pipe along the wall, would have conveyed his meaning quite adequately. I locked the bike to it and struggled up the stairs into one of the lounges. He had definitely been eating garlic or something, and was obviously conscious of it, because as I turned to check the bike, he had his hand up to his face as if smelling his breath. He must have found his scent agreeable since he appeared to be smiling.

The word "Truckline" when applied to the Ferry from Poole is in my opinion a misnomer, for anyone who has ever travelled on one, will tell you how luxurious they are. At that time of night this boat, "The Barfleur", was almost empty, and instead of claiming a seat and sticking to it for fear of never finding another, I roamed about a bit trying to find a fast-food outlet. That half mile ride from the station to the dock had really taken it out of me, and it was now about an hour since my fish and chips. I needed a little rest and maybe something to eat and drink. It was a good job I was going to get trim; this cycling was harder than I remembered.

Another little snackette was purchased and in the process of being digested, I felt the gentle movement of the ship and went to the rail as the large vessel pulled smoothly away and into a harbour which must be the prettiest in the world. It is a sort of pear shape with a narrow opening at the top of the pear across which a little car ferry pulled by chains operates. It takes quite a few minutes sailing to get to the harbour mouth and during that time you get the most glorious views of the lights of the coast and the coast road. Just outside the ferry lane, there are yachts and small dinghies moored for the night, dipping, and nodding to their larger sister, like courtiers bowing to a Queen. We followed the deep channel, but even that is still shallow enough for ships to still touch bottom. In the darkness, the small vessels seemed to me to be moored opposite their respective houses, where the rich and retired resided. It seemed strange that such a large ship could be passing so close to land.

As we passed the dark bulk of Brownsea Island, where Baden Powell developed the Scout movement, I could see the narrow gap, where the chain car ferry crosses the entrance. It seemed impossible that the ship could get through, but passing the "Haven Hotel", where the late diners would be finishing their meal, looking out of the brilliantly lit windows at our passage, we turned towards our destination. I remembered residing in that same hotel, over a period of 4 weeks, sitting in a large sparsely furnished room at its rear, marking hundreds of Police examination papers with 20 or so colleagues. We collated the results, checked, re-checked, and finally wrote down the mark awarded. I apologise to all the officers who feel their senior management are useless. Some of them are there because of me. Equally, you senior officers may be where you are because of my mistake, not because of your skill. What a superb hotel it was though! Out of season, the place was virtually ours, the outdoor pool, the indoor spa baths and steam rooms, gymnasium, 5-star menu and service. I just hope those Sergeants I passed to Inspector, realise how I suffered for them. Perhaps it was watching the ferry pass each night én route for Cherbourg, which gave me the idea for my trip?

As we cleared the buoy and passed into the open sea, the lights of Bournemouth, then the Isle of Wight sparkled, but as they grew fainter, I decided to find a recliner, and have a doze in preparation for my first morning on foreign soil. 5am would soon come.

.

Chapter Three

I don't know whether it was the slight shuddering of the slowing engines, or the noises of people waking up around me, but suddenly it was 04:45am, the passage had come and gone without incident, and we were approaching Cherbourg Harbour. I decided that I would ensure I was one of the first few off, to get out of the way of anyone new to driving on the right, and to get a head start out of the port. The same crew member was waiting for me, and clearly impressed with the indomitable spirit of the English, he had gathered some of his friends nearby. I undid the bike from the piping, as I worked, I could feel his eyes boring into my back. I turned and saw that he was scrutinising me closely. Nothing was said. He began at the white hat, then worked down past the jogging top, shoulder holster, very baggy trousers, trainers, then worked back up again until he arrived at the large belly, the red rimmed eyes, and the round unshaven face. One black eyebrow lifted questioningly with a life of its own as his eyes finished their examination. He spoke slowly as if to a child, and now that he was in his home port, he spoke with a deep resonant French accent. What a transformation from the one he reserved for the tourists! "Vacances?" "Yes, holidays 5 or 6 weeks" I replied. He seemed surprised that an Englishman could respond in his language and flashed back "Et votre transport, c'est ca?" "Yes, the bike, that's all I've got, I'm going on a Tour of France." A mixture of emotions played over his face. On reflection, his response was probably caused by a combination of my totally wrong tense of the verb "To go", in conjunction with the words "Tour de France" and second, the fact that I was a 22 stone Englishman on a bike, arriving in France at a time when they organise that special cycle race.

He exploded into laughter! His face split under his dark moustache! "Tour de France!! Mes Amis, Mes Amis." he gestured to his mates, and went into such a babble of high-speed French I had no chance of achieving a translation. I had no problem getting the message from his hands, however. They outlined my girth, the size of my stomach, the bike, his interpretation of me in the race on the bike, while all the time, the other crew men rolled about singing "Allez Anglais". If anyone ever tells you that the French are a taciturn lot who never smile, I know a Truckline ferry crew who can prove them wrong. Still, it got me off the boat first.

As the ramps lowered, the word had clearly passed down the length of the truck deck. English horns tooted, French ones blared, one set even played the opening strains of Colonel Bogey, and to cheers, or was it hoots of derision? I cycled onto French soil. At least I had the last word in this tactical battle. It was after all my backside the crew were left looking at, as I pedalled unsteadily away.

The port of Cherbourg has been refurbished since my

21

trip, at least the Terminal has. In fact, I witnessed the opening of the new terminal about a week after I arrived, or to put it another way, on the day I returned home! However, that morning, cycling off the boat, it was still dark, and nothing was open as far as I could see. There was, however, a line of little men looking official, all waving the disembarking traffic in one direction. Unfortunately, there were even more little men, looking just as official, who seemed to be pointing the traffic in the opposite direction. I presume that they had turned up to fish off the pier and had decided they would have a bit of fun with "Les Anglais".

It must have been the fishermen, who directed me across, into, and along, the old rail tracks and tramlines, which seemed to be everywhere on the surface of the docks. They had little effect on the cars and lorries, but they certainly affected me. Every jolt and bump were transmitted through the frame of the old bike, into another, softer, old frame, just as if the large, padded saddle wasn't even there. The rather inefficient dynamo hadn't improved since Poole, and as every pothole, rut, and raised chunk of metal welcomed me to the country, the sudden shock of each jolt was magnified by its unexpectedness in the darkness. The official wavers by this time, seeing the fun the fishermen were having, now joined in the game, and from having been first off the boat, I was surprised to find that I had travelled in a circle, and had returned to it, in time to see the last car disappearing into the distance. Dawn was now breaking, and ignoring the pointers and wavers, who by now, being able to see me, were indicating that I was on my second lap, I headed for the main road.

Amazing! with the growing light, I discovered that there were some sections of smooth tarmac between the holes.

There were of course lots of cars and lorries, waiting to return home to England queued up waiting to re-board, many of them clearly surprised by the sight of me approaching out of the greying dawn. I got my final wave from the driver of a Vauxhall car, "H" reg. I think, who obviously believed me to be a returning French onion seller, may have been requesting 2 bunches.

If you've ever been to Cherbourg, there are 2 ways out of the town. One, the old road, is about 2 or 3 miles long, and takes you through the Town, winding up to the top of the cliffs overlooking the port. The climb begins almost as soon as you get to the end of the straight road which takes you away from the port exit gate. I decided against cycling uphill so early in the morning. I took the alternative route, turning left, along the flat sea front, towards a flat road housing estate, where it was peaceful and calm, and one can get used to being on the wrong side of the road. I kept in mind the fact that no matter what manoeuvre you do on French roads, you should always end up with the gutter on your right, and away I went, along these flat roads, happy in the confirmation of my impression that I could cycle all day if they were all like this, beautifully flat!

I passed by several little local shops, recognised a few brand names, crossed a few junctions, "Bon Joured" a few people, it was going to be a fine day. The sun was up, and I even had enough breath to whistle as I rode. I should have saved my breath. A bend appeared, and around that bend, a traffic island, and on the opposite side of that was the dual carriageway from hell. The Cherbourg bypass! This did not wind like the old road which with hindsight, I should have taken. True there were no bends, and it was flat, but the flatness was in a vertical direction. It went straight up in one continuous strip of tarmac. No shops, no seats, no lay-bys, just a very steep, one in something hill.

There was no alternative, it had to be climbed. When we British are in trouble, it's then that our true spirit displays itself. I am proud to say that I did not let the Old Country down. I straightened my shoulders, adjusted the panniers, stood for a moment contemplating what lay before me, and head held high, hair blowing in the wind, I started pushing!

You may have formed the impression that I am a pretty poor cyclist, what with the trailer to my house, then to the station, then the train to Poole etc, and you may well be right in that impression, but I tell you what! You won't see a better pusher!

I could push for England, and believe me, I think I did, trudging up that hill. The first few blasts of continental air horns, (which seemed to have a natural sneering tone), I studiously ignored. I waved my hand in that circular motion favoured by the Royal Family, in the hope that the drivers might just be in doubt as to who they had blared at. It wasn't working. I swear the crew of that damned ferry had passed the word just before going off shift. It seemed as if the whole of Cherbourg was intent on using the by-pass, to see the "Nutty Englishman" and greet him with a toot on the horn. I couldn't wave at all of them, and besides, as the climb steepened and the sun grew hotter, I needed both hands to push. If I let go for a moment with one hand or the other, the bike skewed left or right. The opposite handlebar then dug me in the side and the pedals clipped my ankles. Whose stupid idea was it for me to cycle around France?......

It was now about 9:30am and I was still within 3 miles of Cherbourg, which I could now see, spread out before me. It was a beautiful view and I gazed longingly at the ferries leaving the port én route to England. At this rate I would need about 6 years to complete my trip. Now, if I had brought the car as someone had previously suggested, I dared not dwell on that thought, for as King Lear said, "That way doth madness lie", she couldn't possibly have been right, could she?

The sweat was literally pouring off me, and the clothes, which had seemed appropriate at home, now seemed restrictive in the extreme. They were soaking, my feet ached, my head was boiling in what by now was a really fierce sun, and I needed a long refreshing drink. The road began to level out and there, only a few hundred yards distant, was the island at the top of the by-pass. I got back on and cycled towards it.

Chapter Four

I decided to ignore the main road to Breuville, and took a side road off the island, hoping that I would stand a better chance of finding a house, café, or someplace where I could get a drink. Also, if I wanted to get off and walk again, I could do so in peace and quiet. Anyway, it was in the quiet lanes I would find these accommodating farmers whom I had come to see.

My first piece of good luck! for within a couple of hundred yards off the side road, was a little lane, with a downhill slope which continued for about a mile. I freewheeled down it and came to a tiny village of about 6 houses at most, plus of course the obligatory church. It was the most wonderful place I had seen in France up to that point! It had a roadside toilet! French travellers will know that you rarely, if ever, find a roadside toilet, except in really big towns, and if you do, it is unlikely you would use it as such, much less drink from any tap you ever found in it. BUT there was a brand new convenience under construction in this tiny place. It gleamed, it shone, and it had a large tap, presumably for the workers to use for cement etc. It had no doors and looked a bit like a bus shelter, but it looked great to me.

That water was just like champagne. I drank, put my head under the tap, drank some more, and just sat down on the grass and revelled in the coolness. Where seconds before had been heat and discomfort, all was now wet and happy bliss. When I go back, (in the car) I'll put up one of those roadside plaques to the builders of Le Bosquet, who didn't bother to turn off that tap at the mains, before they went home. Conveniently for me!

As I lay there, I became aware of children's voices unmistakably going through some chanting litany, such as children do all round the world, when being tested by a teacher. It wasn't 2 and 2 are 4, but it was something similar. I had a final drink and began to stiffen up in most of my muscles and joints, mounted up and cycled off. A left turn and a short lane later, the source of the chanting was identified as coming from a school room, which was exactly that! One room, a small playground and nothing else. I could see the children inside, and that little place seemed to me at that moment, to epitomise England's past. How I envied them being taught in such a perfect spot. They looked happy, and the sun and the countryside were just a door away.

It was hard to believe that I was still less than 5 miles from Cherbourg, it felt as if I was in the heart of rural France. I suppose I was, in terms of attitude, for the ports and tourist traps, seem to want your money but not your conversation. The residents there can in the main speak better English than you can speak French and seem to want to move to the next day tripper buying his quota and ring up the till. What a difference those few miles had made. One little lad saw me looking and waved at me, a second followed suit. I waved back and the next minute, I saw the teacher speaking to them both and for a second thought that their friendly gesture had got them both into trouble. The door opened and an official voice asked "What did I want? Was there a problem?"

I replied with my prepared script about retirement and travelling in France and being English, and wanting to speak French better, and the next minute, all the children had been called out by her into the yard to talk to me. I am ashamed to say that they spoke so quickly I could hardly understand them, in their native language, but their English was very good and precise. I suppose I was there for about 10 minutes, talking about "school in England" and "Where did I live?" in a mixture of both languages, as words and expressions came or went from me. With lots of waving and good-byes the teacher shooed them back inside. They were too polite to laugh at my efforts, but I got the impression that my spoken French could improve. Perhaps I was the first Englishman they had spoken to. I could see how that might have been a shock to an impressionable small child. I dare say that if I had seen a large Frenchman on a bike, who spoke awful English, when I was little, I might have smiled too. In any case, I was waved off by the whole school, all 20 of them, and despite my aching legs, had to keep on pedalling until I got out of sight, it wouldn't have done to have them see me get off within a few feet.

Around the next bend the lane became a tunnel overhung with trees and then suddenly, it burst out again into the sunlight and I realised that I had gone round in an arc, bypassing the main road. There were no alternative roads. The D 900 to Breuville it was.

To be honest, it was all right. By now it was about 11am and traffic was relatively light as it seems to be in France on the

"A" roads. I suppose most of the heavy stuff makes for the motorways as it does here. Whatever the reason, with the road being reasonably level and no hooting every few seconds to frighten you into a speed wobble, (I use the word speed advisedly), I was quite enjoying my journey.

Unsurprisingly, to you the reader, at the first sign of an incline, (which had just appeared), I dismounted and began to push. Almost instantly both of my thigh muscles went into a severe cramp. Thinking that stopping cycling had been the cause, I tried to start again, but there was no chance. I massaged and pummelled to no avail; it was simply a question of letting it gradually wear off. As I sat there on the verge, with my back to a large stone wall, I heard the sound of someone muttering and the chink of stones against metal. I hobbled to my feet and set in the wall about 10 feet away was a large gate which I hopped up to and looked over.

Chapter Five

The equivalent of a Devon Yokel, Country Gaffer, Wurzel Gummidge and Steptoe, all rolled into one, but clearly and distinctly French, was raking a vegetable patch and talking to himself. He was incredibly dirty, both in clothing and personally, and looked as if he had recently gone three rounds with some pigs and lost. He saw me and began to speak. It could have been Martian for all I understood. First the children, now an octogenarian. When would I find a native who would speak slowly enough for me understand fully first time? I begged his pardon and said that I would appreciate it if he spoke slowly, after all I was English.

I had said the magic word! His face lit up! "English", he said again and again and off he went fifteen to the dozen. His gestures, and the odd word I could understand were clearly inviting me into the farm. I heard the word "drink" and followed, pleased at the prospect of further refreshment. We walked from the garden patch into a small three-sided courtyard, and there facing us, was what I took to be a barn door. It was enormous! It stood the full height of the wall and about 10 feet wide, a typical barn door. Huge hinges, massive bolts, knot holes so big you could put your fingers in them. The only strange thing about it was the presence of an antiquated lock, which I have to say I felt was a bit over the top. What could there be of value in the place that needed a lock.? The elderly gent looked unkempt, the yard and outbuildings were even worse. In the yard corner was a large rusty pump from which water was dribbling into a stone sink on two barrels. The only thing missing were animals.

Just for a moment my plans altered. If the old boy was the owner, then if I stopped here for the whole of my holiday, I could help him tidy it up. Mind you, I had doubts as to whether my French would improve with him as a teacher.

As we reached the door, he produced a large "dungeon" type key, and opening it, beckoned me to follow into the shadowy interior. Should Hammer Horror ever produce pictures again, I have a perfect set for them. The door creaked on cue, and the temperature dropped several degrees as I entered. I began to wonder if anyone had seen me go in and would I be missed? It wasn't a barn at all! On the wall opposite me was a huge fireplace, the chimney of which projected out about 3 feet. In the space either side of the fireplace were 2 alcoves. Inside each of them, raised up from the floor about 3 feet, was a bed, and hanging down from the ceiling were curtains which could clearly be drawn around to keep out the draught.

The room, which was about 35 feet by 15 feet, was living room, dining room, kitchen, bedroom, and general workplace, and was scattered with every conceivable household and living implement you could imagine. A scythe hanging from one wall was the only thing I recognised at first glance, but it looked as if everything he had ever owned from the year dot to the present day was there. As my eyes adjusted to the light from two windows, which I now noticed, high in the wall and either side of the door, I could see that one of the alcove beds was beautifully made up. The bedspread was stretched tight, the pillows plumped up, and on the rear wall, was a picture of a stern faced woman. The colour of the linen indicated that it had been untouched for many years. The second was rumpled and downright dirty and looked as if it too had remained untouched (at least by soap and water). I made a guess that his wife had used the made up one, and that after her death, he had preserved it like a little shrine to her. As he fished in and out of draws and cupboards around the room, it was clear, that despite its dirt and grime, the furniture and many of the fittings were superbly carved.

I drew on the vast experience I had gained over the last few years of watching The Antiques Roadshow and decided that they were valuable. A large standing clock, like a grandfather clock but with the casing open and a beautifully painted pear-shaped pendulum took my eye. I also liked the look of a dresser type of thing which was very ornate. His shout made me jump as he produced from a draw, a flat case as big as the palm of your hand. He opened it and displayed three medals. I have no idea what they were, but tucked into the flap was a photo of a man of about 25 or 30, and a woman of the same sort of age, standing either side of a British soldier. It had to be my host and his wife.

Off he went again, gesticulating at the picture, the medals, laughing at some long-forgotten joke, then back to the medals, and gradually, I pieced the rapid words together. Two of the medals were French, and I think were his fathers from the Great War. The other was English. He had exchanged the third of his Fathers medals with one the soldier had, to commemorate the Liberation after the Second World War. They had made the usual promises one to another about coming back etc. etc. but it had come to nothing. Now, here I was, with the 50th anniversary of D-Day only a few days passed, "It was fate. I must have a drink."

"All right", I said, "I'll have a drink", but with the heat and the fact that I hadn't eaten since the snack on the boat, I insisted that it should be water. I felt really bad, the poor old soul was obviously lonely, and it did seem to be less than generous to decline. However, drinking either a rough wine or local brandy, might have meant a quick trip to the local gendarmerie, and that was an embarrassment I could do without.

"Just water?" He seemed a little puzzled with my choice. He picked up a bottle and clearly intended to drink from it, so he was catered for, but his range of utensils for me, seemed rather limited. He handed me a tin cup which could well have belonged to the same soldier who swapped him the medal, it could have been aged by the rings inside it. As I looked at it, trying to work out when I had last been injected for tetanus, he began to walk towards his bed.

At that moment I realised that I could see no tap or sink within the room. He lifted a fold of a dirty sheet which had drooped from his bed overnight, and as I watched in horror, reached under the bed, and began to feel around. I froze! I remember thinking, I did say water, didn't I? Perhaps water has another meaning in his local dialect? No wonder he looked puzzled when I insisted on having water. I heard the unmistakable chink of China against bed springs. If he came out from under that bed with anything remotely like a chamber pot, I was off, cramp or not! As if in slow motion, into the light, clutched in his grimy hand, came a tall antique looking, swan necked jug, brilliantly painted with flowers, with a lace cover weighted at the corners, covering the top. I breathed an audible sigh of relief. Its shape proclaimed the impossibility of anything unsanitary being in it. I couldn't have aimed into that swan neck in the dark in the middle of the night, never mind this ancient Frenchman.

He poured out some of its contents into the tin mug. It was indeed water! Fresh and clean. "Cold" he was saying, "under the bed was cold." Cold and clean it might have been but pouring it into that tin cup changed one of those characteristics immediately, as the level rose over the "Rings".

"Go on drink" he said.

I put the thing to my mouth. The longer I put off the moment, the more the encrusted rings softened up, allowing more bits to float into the solution. I had to drink it soon before it changed from minestrone soup to thick stew. I gagged it down feeling my stomach wanting to reject it. All thoughts of stopping here for the duration of my holiday had disappeared in the face of that insanitary tin cup. My mind was ablaze with the variety of utensils on which he could serve food, multiplied by the cleanliness factor of each and every one, or rather the lack of the same. He was a very nice, friendly French gentleman, and should he ever read this I hope he will understand, but he must have heard of culture shock, and I didn't intend to suffer from the sort of culture I could have found in that farmhouse.

I bade him "A tout a l'heure" and backing out of the "barn" cramp forgotten, recovered the bike, and set off again.

I swear it was no more than 500 yards from the farm, that

I reached the crossroads. On one corner was a small café, and on the other a general store. In the café I had a carton of milk from a sterilized, homogenized, decontaminated, computerized waxed carton. In the general stores I bought a packet of biscuits and some crisps. All of which were untouched by human hand. If only I had had the strength to travel those extra few yards, I needn't have suffered. Still, the water did me no apparent harm, unless you count memory loss. I left my hat in the café, and by the time I realised it, I was too far away to think about going back to get it.

Chapter Six

I carried straight on, still heading towards my first goal in France, the town of Bricquebec-en-Cotentin, and hoping to get there before the late afternoon. I seemed to have got over some sort of ridge near the coast, and from the elevated position I was in, it looked pretty much downhill. I struggled on, stopping about 2pm, in a small place, the name of which, Rauville la Bigot, was totally justified, bearing in mind what later happened, and bought 50 grams of superb "terrine", a small French stick, and some milk. I put the bike against the wall of the shop and sat down on the concrete with my back to the shop wall at its side.

The concrete felt softer than the saddle. As I sat there eating and drinking the milk, I became the subject of the law which states that "Strangers stand out like sore thumbs". Hence also the name La Bigot. I must have dozed off but woke with a start to see a Policeman on a motor bike, just pulling up.

I imagined the call, "Yes officer, a big fat man, fast asleep, may be drunk, no, never seen him before, one hand holding a bike and the other a half-eaten baguette."

Here he came, approaching in the traditional way of all

motorcycle officers, slightly swaggering as if his engine was still running, and hands on hips.

I have always respected the law, being an ex-policeman. Believe me, when you are in a foreign country, where police officers wear guns and are walking towards you, you respect them even more! I waited till he had settled himself in front of me so that he would not misinterpret any sudden moves, and for the first time realized that wearing a leather wallet which looked like a shoulder holster, might not be a good idea. What a depth of meaning there can be in the single word "Monsieur?" when addressed to you by a Police Officer with a gun, in the middle of France. I translated it quite specifically as, "Get up slowly you tub of lard, or I will shoot you and then search your body for your papers". So, I did just that, and carefully struggled to my feet, pointing at my empty fingers of my right hand with my left hand, I smiled sickeningly, extracted my passport, and handed it over.

It was examined, and then with an upward nod of the head which obviously meant "Got anything else?" he handed it back to me. I produced my trump card, wondering why I hadn't thought of it before. My card! It simply said that as an ex-officer, I was permitted to enter Police buildings, but it was official, and had Police written on it. He inspected it, and taking advantage of still being alive, I went into my spiel about retirement from high police positions, and holidays etc. He said nothing, handed back the folded card, put his gun in his holster, saluted and drove away. I imagined his report to Headquarters.

"No problem, it's that fat Englishman from this morning's ferry. That's right, he hasn't got very far, but I don't think he'll last long".

The adrenaline generated by this encounter had removed all my aches and pains! I wondered if terrifying patients was a legitimate means of curing the sick? and did that officer know he had the power to do it? Equally strange was the fact that a few seconds earlier, it seemed that he and I had been the only ones in the village. Now, people were moving around again. I felt like saying "Which one of you ******** dropped me in it?", but with as much dignity as I could muster, I mounted the bike and pedalled off. In the excitement, I had completely forgotten Ron's explanatory letter. Good job, it probably was as wet as the money and unreadable.

The adrenaline rush lasted long enough for me go three or four miles without stopping and at about 4pm, I arrived at Breuville, cycling in, I stopped at a small Post Office on the edge of the village. I asked the lady if she could give me change "Pour telephoner". You may recall I had been wearing a sort of shoulder holster thing with all my valuables in it. She looked at what once had been a crisp 100 Franc note, and gingerly picked up the damp piece of paper it had now become, having absorbed the essence that was England from somewhere near my armpit. I think she wanted to refuse to take it, but it was legal tender and so perhaps she couldn't. "I want to phone my wife" I said. It was that I think, that made her feel sorry for me. She handed me some notes and a pile of large coins slightly bigger than a 50p piece, and out I went to the phone box.

I told my wife where I was and my general condition, she made the usual wifely noises. I said I would ring again when I arrived at my campsite.

As I lifted my leg to traverse the crossbar, I noticed the saddle! It was a plastic composite stretched over springs, (which I had been assured, at the partially sighted school in Harborne, would be adequate), it was deteriorating. You didn't have to be blind (pardon the bad joke) to see that the cover was pulling back from the pointed end of the saddle and a spring was poking out. It might have been tested in the laboratory, but it hadn't been under the rear end of a considerable weight, to wit, my backside, for several hours. I didn't blame the school for selling it to me, or indeed the makers, they just hadn't catered for the stupidity factor of the purchaser. This did not bode well for the remaining 5 weeks and 5 days of my cycling tour if the saddle was dying after less than a day.

To add insult to injury, as I stood there, a French cyclist crested the brow of the slight incline up which I had just pushed my bike. He was sun bronzed and muscled in places long forgotten by me. He wasn't even sweating, he just shone, as if freshly oiled. He threw his lightweight racing cycle from side to side as he pushed the big gears with effortless ease. There was a whoosh of air as he sped past with a sneering glance at me. I bet both he and the bike together didn't weigh as much as my left leg! I hated him instantly! How I hoped to find him wrapped around a tree in the next mile. Needless to say, I didn't even have that satisfaction, but strangely enough considering that "Le Tour" was soon to happen, and the popularity of cycling in France, he was the only cyclist I saw on my trip.

I didn't remain dispirited for long however, for I pictured myself, in 6 weeks' time, lithe, brown, athletic, and powerful. Just let him try to pass me on the way back!

Chapter Seven

I was there! I crested a small rise and there was Bricquebec-en-Cotentin. As I freewheeled down the road towards it, I remembered last time I had seen it 3 years ago. We were coming home from a driving holiday and decided to stop for some lunch, intending to drive on to Cherbourg to stay there overnight and catch the early ferry.

When we drove in it was clear some sort of a fair was taking place. There was a cattle sale in the big square behind the Chateau, the metal corrals full of cows, pigs, sheep, chickens, and the farm lorries all around the perimeter, still loading or unloading. There were joints of meat being roasted on portable ovens, like the ones on which you roast potatoes. There were roundabouts and an organ, and a play being performed in the grounds of the Chateau itself, and a general air of "Frenchness" which is indescribable. What really caught our eye, or should I say ear, was a strange buzzing noise coming from within a crowd of people on the corner by the camera shop.

As you drive into the town from the coast and the direction of Barneville-Carteret, the long straight road, as indeed many are in France, leads you directly up to the entrance of the Chateau. There the road branches left and right on either side of it. On the left corner is the camera shop and outside it was the reason for the buzzing. A man was carving pieces from a 6 feet high tree trunk. Unusual? No, except he was carving it with chain saws. He had about four different sizes of saws, ranging from large down to a tiny one which almost fitted in his hand. He would start the required size saw, make a few deft movements, a few comments to the crowd, a puff on a soggy cigar, protruding from underneath a grey but nicotine stained moustache, then a few more cuts. Whatever he was carving, he had only just begun, and it was impossible to decide what it was.

We stayed and watched him for a few minutes, then decided that we would come back after something to eat so we found a place to buy bread, cheese, some pate and fruit, and parking up by the cattle market and fair, we ate our lunch.

About an hour later, we walked through the grounds of the Chateau, and listened to the players on their improvised stage. I hope it doesn't seem too anti-French, but it was exactly as I had imagined French plays to be. Very serious and lots of deep, brooding silences, accompanied by dark drab clothing and many, many gestures. The audience reflected the nature of the piece, watching quietly and clearly pondering on the meaning of life. It was either that, or the actors were putting in the silences because they were forgetting their lines. I sat on a wall and had a chat with a local who must have thought a foreigner slightly more interesting than the play. He did ask "If I was enjoying this famous comedy?". I can only presume that with a serious drama, they cry less. I recommend any Punch and Judy man who thinks there might be a niche market in

France, not to bother. We looked in through the windows of the town museum, housed in the chateau gatehouse. It was closed but walking through the gate brought us back to the camera shop.

In that hour, the chain saw man had carved well, for you could see that he was shaping the tree into the form of a knight in armour. The knight held a sword in one hand, while the other arm was hidden behind the shield, the point of which rested on the floor. The crowd had grown smaller, and getting closer, I managed to ask someone nearby, who was the man and why was he carving the tree?

I was subjected to a torrent of rapid French which after about 5 minutes I managed to work out as follows.

The man was a famous sculptor in France and had shown his work all over the country. In the large rooms to our right there was apparently an exhibition of his work, and because he was present at this fete, he was offering the carving for sale, to boost a charity appeal.

My wife and I went round the exhibition and sure enough, there were actual pieces, and pictures of the chap standing beside other sculptures, taken in different parts of France. I am sorry to say I didn't know him, had never heard of him, and didn't really like his work, but I was interested in buying the carving he was currently making. The cross on the shield and the style, was that of a Knight Templar, and I had it in mind to present it to a society, interested in that era, of which I am a member.

Returning to the site, the work was almost complete in rough form. It obviously needed a lot more work from the finishing point of view, sanding and smoothing etc, but it was a lovely piece of work. It was equally obvious that I could not take it with me there and then because of the need for its completion, and its sheer size. We had after all, come for a holiday, not to buy half a tree. Nevertheless, I spoke to the artist, and asked him what price he wanted? I was delighted when he said only £100, something like a 1000 Francs at that time. There was a problem, because for that price, I had to take it now, as it was. He was sure that "there were craftsman who could finish it in England", but he was returning south that evening, and he considered his work done. "Pas un problem" for him, but there was for me. There was no way that I could get it in my car.

I asked whether he could arrange for it to be kept locally for me, while I made arrangements to have it brought over? "Non!" it had to be now or never. To my regret, it had to be never. He expressed his sorrow and said that he would present it to the Town for them to sell it. Now 3 years later I was returning, and I remembered with some annoyance, the circumstances which had prevented me bringing that piece of carving home.

Chapter Eight

There was the sign on the edge of the town, and I gratefully freewheeled into the large area behind the Chateau, where the cattle market had been held. There is a sort of one-way system around the Chateau, and where it joins the market square, there are 2 cafés on either side of the road. The tourist information office is on the opposite side of the square from a little hotel called "Le Donjon". It seemed very quiet, no doubt because by now it was well into the eighties, so I went into the tourist office to enquire about a campsite.

A pretty young lady of about 17 was in charge, but regretfully her information ended a perfect day. The nearest campsite was on a small farm, run by a Mr & Mrs Begin, but it was on the Bricquebec-en-Cotentin to Valognes road, the D902, roughly at right angles to the road I had arrived on and about 2 miles away. It was the last straw! My legs felt like jelly, I was hot, tired, aching, stiff, hungry, and for the first time in about 37yrs I had cycled about 20 miles in a day, I couldn't go any further. I was done! If I had wanted to move at that moment it would have been impossible. So, I sat, and we talked.

She spoke excellent English and was still at college,

earning a few francs by acting as a tourist officer. She was very polite, and after my initial introduction, she allowed me to speak French, and hardly laughed when I told her of my plans. She even complimented my accent and gave me the name of the café owner next door, so that I could get a large cup of coffee in the English style. I couldn't see how knowing and using his Christian name, influenced the strength of his brew, but again it was probably my translation.

I was too tired to care what anyone thought of my sweaty clothes, my battered old bike with its panniers and elastic straps and the even more battered rider. I bid her goodbye and went next door.

"Café" I said in a snappish voice, born from tiredness "Et un cognac".

Within seconds, both drinks were served, no comment was made, no small talk, just service and silence. I hadn't even tried his name. The method was clear. Although obviously not French, I had displayed enough attitude to indicate that I didn't want to be disturbed, and that anyone who did disturb me would get the rough edge of my tongue. I might have to resort to this tactic again.

I really didn't want to move, but I still had to locate the site. I could no longer put off the inevitable, so bidding farewell to the owner, I re- mounted, and wearily pushed the pedals round, out of the town. Thank God the information lady was bad on distances. It was only about a kilometre to the turn off she had described. A turn right into the lane then right again into the farm drive, I was there! I pushed the bike over the ruts towards the farmhouse.

It was in an "L" shape, the long part being the main house with a barn at one end, from where I could hear cows. The short end was a lean to, with tractors and machinery inside. To the left was a small clump of trees with a path through them into a field. The main gate to the field was right in front of me and I pushed the bike towards it.

There was a sign in several languages saying "Go on in and camp and someone will see you later".

The field was empty except for one caravan, which seemed unoccupied. I went no more than 30 yards or so, undid the elastic ropes, dropped my bundles on the grass and leant the bike against the hedge. I knew that if I didn't get the tent up and gear out, I would just fall asleep on the grass, so praying that the rods and ropes would give me no trouble, I started. It was as easy as the instructions said, and I mentally thanked all my colleagues who had voted to get me something simple, even if it was because they thought I couldn't cope with complicated things. Literally within 3 minutes it was done, and I was laying out everything inside it. A few minutes passed, when a discreet cough introduced the farmer's wife, whose name I later learnt was Jacqueline, like that of my wife. In rapid French she said something, and then pointed at the shower block. After a day of sweating, drying, sweating again etc, I suppose I may have been rather noticeable, but I didn't need the hint. With towel and shampoo in hand, I almost crawled across the grass towards the showers to ease my aching limbs.

I must praise France for its control of camp sites, for if they are registered nationally, then the minimum standards are rigorously enforced. You are even invited to complain to the local authorities if you are dissatisfied. The effect of the registration is that even on the smallest farm, the facilities are great. Here was no exception. There were washing bowls, flush toilets, hot and cold showers, drinking water taps and everything was spotlessly clean. I went into a cubicle, stripped, and luxuriated in the best shower I have ever had. Cold, Warm, Hot, Warm, Cold. It was marvellous. I wrapped the towel around me (it was a big towel) and examined the bruises I had already gained. There was a beauty across the whole width of my stomach, where the handlebars had loosened and dropped down, dropping me with them, and I suspected my backside was just as colourful.

I had been back in the tent about 15 minutes, and I had had time to change into shorts and spread most of my sweaty clothes over the tent, to dry, when Yves-Marie (Mr. Begin) appeared offering milk, fresh bread, cheese, and a couple of hard-boiled eggs. They were really lovely people, and that simple meal took some beating I can tell you.

By 8:30pm, my wet clothes had dried in the late afternoon sun, and despite the fact that I had no sleeping bag, I was so tired and pleasantly full, that, re-clothed, I rolled up a dry towel as a pillow, and dropped straight off to sleep. I suppose I snored, I usually do, but there was no-one to complain. I awoke once in the night, something French was snuffling its way round the tent, I rose, walked over to the toilets, and when I came out saw the most superb night sky. No city lights to hide the stars, no clouds, no moon to speak of, just a black velvet cloth scattered with millions of diamonds. I stood for several minutes, watching shooting stars and tracing the Milky Way, then poetic license had to go, my feet were getting cold. I went back into the tent and soon dozed off, anticipating the second day of my adventure.

I awoke to what appeared to me, to be a deathly silence. My city ear being attuned to the sound of heavy traffic passing my bedroom on a main road into Birmingham, birdsong through the thin wall of a tent was hardly audible. The earth, which the night before, had seemed so soft and welcoming, had magically changed to the consistency of solid concrete. The bruises in the various parts of my anatomy had grown into fully fledged aches, and I creaked into an upright position. I imagined another 41 such nights before I slept in my bed again, and wondered whether I shouldn't have brought a bed roll after all to soften the blow? It was about 7:30am and the dew was on the grass. I was still the sole tenant of the field, and I paddled across to the shower and toilet block, thinking about breakfast.

Nothing like a lovely hot shower, to breathe life back into an aching body, but it had also sharpened the appetite. There was a small problem however, for in the planning stage at home, where a bacon butty was only as far away as the fridge and cooker, I had made another poor decision. Why take heavy food? when every generous French farmer would provide it. Why take drinks? or even a tiny spirit stove? when I could stop for coffee and croissants at cafés as I passed through local villages. The reality of knowing that I could not even brew up hit me. I could hear that things were stirring in the farm, but not having earned my keep, felt unable to impose on the family's generosity any further.

I decided that I would get dressed, and bike into Bricquebec-en-Cotentin, by which time, somewhere would be open, and after eating, I would buy cornflakes, milk and sugar and a few other staples. No point in journeying on until I had hardened up a bit, and this seemed a good spot for hardening.

The roads were even quieter that second morning, it was very pleasant pedalling back to the little town, at that time of day. At least until, without warning, my legs spun round at a rate of knots, and the knobbly bone on the inside of my right ankle cracked against the pedal as my foot slipped. The chain had broken, and my ankle felt as if it had too. I explained my feelings to the empty road, while dancing around trying to make the pain go away, without success! I could now add a rainbow ankle bone to the collection of coloured body parts I possessed. Time passed and the pain diminished as the swelling grew. "Pas un problem" I said to myself as I scrabbled around in the saddle bag. There they were, among the tyres, bulbs, brake pads, and other bits and pieces, the links for the chain. What planning and foresight. I sat on the roadside, congratulating myself on getting something right, and got to work mending the chain. Those lads in the school for partially sighted hadn't spared the grease, and it was proving rather hard to pull the ends of the chain together and fit the link. In fact, it was impossible, for the realisation suddenly hit me, just as my hands were nicely coated in black gunge, that the links were the wrong size! This time I really let rip! I had more colours than Joseph's coat, I ached everywhere, I wanted a good fry up and a cup of tea, my bike was broken, I was filthy dirty, and what was worse, at this rate, I was never going to get thin and bronzed. The reader will understand, why I believe the first doubts as to my capacity to last 6 weeks were planted just at that moment.

I arrived pushing my bike, at about 08:30am, confident that if nothing else, there was bound to be a cycle shop in Bricquebec-en-Cotentin. There was, but oh what a surprise the shop wasn't open. I would have a coffee while waiting. I looked at myself. Would I serve someone who looked as if he'd slept all night under a truck with a leaky gearbox? I settled down to wait outside the shop. It looked ok. New bikes and accessories filled the window, and right inside I could see, shoes, caps, shirts, and lots of those Lycra shorts so beloved of true cyclists. I waited until about 9:15am and filled my time cleaning my hands on a clump of grass so that when the owner finally arrived, in a car! I was right behind him as he opened the door. If he intended to have a coffee before starting business, I wanted one too. He greeted me with "Huh?" Once again there was that rising inflection at the end which means "Can I help you?" "What do you want?" and a million other things. I didn't know the words for "chain-link" or "it doesn't fit" and so I simply held out my grubby hands, with the link in one and the chain in the other and made a snapping gesture. How much we undemonstrative English lose by not using our hands more in conversation. No more was needed. "Pas un problem?" he said, and as he checked in various boxes, I told him what I was doing, and waited for the laugh. He just smiled, and then looking at my ample form offered me, at a good price, a yellow jersey, and a pair of Lycra shorts to go with the link. I almost asked him if he had a relative who was a crew member on the Barfleur. I might have managed the yellow jersey, but I would never have got one leg in the shorts never mind the important bits. He came outside, looked at the bike, then at my hands, and with practiced ease had the chain re-fitted in a minute or two. I was just about to cycle away when some premonition made me stop and purchase several more links. One never knew! And he had been good enough to mend the chain.

Chapter Nine

I wandered around the little town, pushing or cycling as I felt inclined, and renewed my recollections of my last visit. We had actually stayed in the Hotel within the Chateau, thinking that it would be something to remember. Four poster beds and the Three Musketeers maybe? I remembered it as a corner room, with a wash basin and mirror, separated from the toilet and shower by a 3foot high screen, all jammed into the said corner. The bed had been put in as an afterthought, but it was possible to save time in the morning by shaving as you sat. To be fair, I am sure there were such rooms as we had dreamed of it was just that for 190 Francs, we got the one with "Character". The museum was open, and I took the opportunity of going in. It was full of local exhibits including, beds like the ones in "Steptoe's" barn, the same sort of clock, and there in the corner, was my Knight Templar. It was still in its original, unfinished state, and the only addition to it seemed to be some holes, which had been drilled in the helmet visor. It was not for sale.

I went back to the café by the tourist centre, and the proprietor didn't turn a hair. I suppose that workers and farmers came in from the market looking just as bad, if not worse than me. I had coffee and a "Croque Monsieur" (a toasted sandwich) and went out to stock up. During the shopping I learnt that bacon is called "lard", it's like extra thick belly draft and is used more for flavouring than for its meat content. Also, that you couldn't get any sort of tinned baked beans in France. I bought some salami type sausage, bread, corn flakes, coffee, and fruit, knowing all the dairy products were available at the farm. My best buys I got at a general store, they were a metal frame with a cup under it, on which you placed a small firelighter, and a tin mug. I could now have a brew! Why hadn't I thought of it in England? As I cycled back to the campsite, the word had clearly begun to spread, for a few people waved and "Bonjoured" me. It was warm, I had eaten and had a coffee, and life wasn't so bad. Wrong! About a hundred yards from home, my premonition proved correct. The chain went again in a different place!

And so, the days passed. I would cycle to the Town, stock up, drink in the café, wander about, cycle back, laze around the farm, talk to the children, eat, drink, but most of all, the chain would keep breaking, and I would buy links for it! I was now well known in Bricquebec-en-Cotentin. Indeed, I believe that were I to go back now, mothers would bring out their children and say "The Nutty Englishman has returned. You remember, the one who made the cycle shop owner a rich man buying links, when he could have just bought a new chain" In fairness, looking back, I often ask myself that question. Why didn't I buy a chain? Perhaps I knew deep down that I was never going to cycle around France and was looking for an excuse to go home. I had bitten off more than I could chew, and the ground was growing harder by the night. It was a bitter pill to swallow, but as the days passed, I realised that my wife had got me pegged. It was on about the 5th day I began to formulate excuses for returning early. It was impossible to claim that I had achieved the peak of physical fitness I had set for myself, for in truth I was in a worse condition than that in which I had left. I was literally black and blue in every place visible to me, and probably everywhere else as well.

In my career in the Force, I had made some hard decisions, and as a father I had made even more, but this was going to be the hardest of my life. Not only was I going to have to suffer the ridicule of my friends and relations, but worse, I was going to have to admit to my wife that I was wrong, and she was right! I should have taken the car. I should have put the bike in the back. I should have trained. I had the answer! All of these things were true, but I could salvage some self-respect. I could have done it, I could have continued entertaining the French populace, the basic idea was a good one and I didn't really want to come home. The injuries meant nothing, the hard ground, the hard saddle, honest, I didn't mind the pain, it was the bike, the bike just wasn't up to it.

Once the decision had been made the rest seemed easy. If I was going home, there seemed little further point in using the bike, so I determined that we would both travel back to Cherbourg by train saving further difficulties which might occur on the way. On my next visit to the town, I enquired about train times and the nearest station. It was nearly as far to the station as it was to Cherbourg and not only that, but if I heard properly and translated correctly, the fare would cost me only 20 Francs, but the bike would be about 230. There seemed nothing to be gained in that direction. It looked as if I would have to cycle back the way I had come.

That afternoon, while talking to Mr. Begin about my problem, he told me that he had a friend who regularly went into Cherbourg with his vehicle and that he would arrange for him to give me a lift, bike, equipment, and all. With almost unheard of speed given the normal pace of living, the arrangements were made, and it was agreed that the following morning, the friend would collect me. As I dropped off to sleep later that evening, I looked forward to my return, and mentally rehearsed my excuses. The ferry left at 08:05am Mr. Begin had said that he had to get up at 5:30am to let the cows out of the shed, so "No Problem" he would wake me. His friend would come at about 06:45am, which would leave plenty of time for everything to be packed and ready to go. Wrong!

First problem, the cows were still in the shed, and I didn't get a wakeup call, but thank God, I woke myself at about 6am. I rushed around like a demented idiot packing everything in the panniers, folding the tent, etc. etc. so that I wouldn't be late for the "Friend".

Third problem, it was only the friend's arrival at 7am which finally got Mr. Begin out of bed full of apologies, protesting that we still had sufficient time, but I race ahead of myself, I've missed the second problem.

As I stood fuming by the gate, still waiting for Mr. Begin and his mate to put in an appearance, the friend arrived. As I said, it was now 7am and what an arrival! Through the gate came, not a truck as I had imagined, but a low-slung, soft suspension, Citroen hatch back car. "So what?" I hear you say.

It was white in colour!

"So what?" you may be saying again, and "So what" indeed in normal circumstances, but it was a low-slung white Citroen hatch back for a reason.

It was designed to carry people lying down!

I sense you are tiring of the quiz so here are some clues. On the top was a blue light and in the back was a stretcher. The friend was the driver of a private ambulance, and this was the transport. It could only have been marginally worse by being a hearse. I admit I felt bad enough to justify the vehicle, but this had to be a joke! Just for a second, I wondered if Jacqueline Begin and Jacqueline Weston had been in touch and arranged this final insult. Going home in an ambulance indeed! At least the bike wouldn't die from its wounds. As I stood recovering from shock, Mr. Begin appeared at his door and having only just risen decided that he needed his morning cup of coffee, and generously invited my driver and me to join him. "No problem plenty of time". Apparently, the friend had just finished his night shift, so the coffee was a necessity for him too. Apologies were offered in all directions, but this was a most unusual happening. He was never late getting up. My bowl of coffee had gone but theirs was being savoured. I kept pointedly looking at my watch as 08:05am was getting ever closer, and I still had to book in and get on board. Neither man moved, but both had a knowing smile on their faces, which seemed to say, "Doesn't he understand? we've told him there's no problem!".

I was missing something!

It was 7:30am when realisation dawned. With the coffee finished, a rubber sheet had been placed over the stretcher, and the bike and my possessions laid on top of it. I almost expected the friend, whose name I never had time to establish, to cover them with a blanket. I thanked the Begin family for really looking after their solitary camper. I paid my bill and left some extra francs for presents for the children, and they waved us off. At 7:30am precisely we emerged from the farm track onto the road, and as I said, the reason for their unconcern hit me. The friend reached forward to the dashboard, turned on the blue light and horn, pressed the pedal to the metal and we took off!

Were we a fully authorised emergency vehicle? I never knew! We flew along the straights, we leapt the brows of hills to land bloodied but unbowed 20 feet over the crest, we overtook in the face of oncoming traffic, while with gallic indifference the driver put his elbow on the sill and smoked a cigarette. We never slowed never mind stopped! Junctions, level crossings, traffic lights were all treated with the same contempt, but in the blur, I swear I saw mothers with babies throwing themselves into hedges, and priests genuflecting for the soul of the poor unfortunate inside the passing ambulance.

It wasn't the naked terror which bothered me, though looking back I wouldn't care to repeat the journey. My real concern was the prospect of a Police Patrol deciding to escort us and finding a dying English cycle as a patient. Even worse, what if it was the officer from Le Bigot. Even Ron's explanatory letter and my card wouldn't have got me out of the local Police station.

As we sped towards Cherbourg, the friend, kept up a steady flow of chatter, taking his hand from the wheel to gesture to various interesting places. I just kept thinking, we'll get there on time or die trying. Probably the latter. Wrong! It was a pointless exercise, for despite the siren, light, and best efforts of the driver to kill us both, we had left it too late! The ferry was just pulling away from the quayside, puffing little rings of exhaust from its funnels. I knew the next one was much later that day and that it would be a close call on catching the Birmingham train at Bournemouth as a result. One thing was certain, I was going to spend at least another half a day in France, "Pas un flaming Problem". Oh Really!

Chapter Ten

Although there was now no need, we screeched to a halt, the two tones slowing dying, at the doors of a shiny new building, which I later learnt was the new terminal. Interested bystanders and prospective passengers watched, as a terminal employee rushed towards us, intent on getting his name in the papers, but he withdrew, with a dirty French word when he saw the true situation. The driver and I dragged out the patient, I handed over about 100 Francs, and scattering the gravel, he roared off. As soon as the little crowd realised there was no blood they drifted away, while I leant the bike against the crash barriers secured it and went inside. The place was absolutely brand new. Along both sides of the hall were booths for the various shipping and car hire companies. There was a sort of gallery across the centre, and at the far end a snack bar with an upper terrace, where you could sit and watch the ships entering and leaving the port. I hadn't seen this building when I arrived in the dark of the morning, but I had come at just the right time of day to see it officially opened. Everywhere you could see, there was tricolour ribbon. French flags were hung over a grand arch which had been created by great loops of cloth hanging from the central gallery, and in the gallery were seats and music stands.

I enquired at the Brittany ferries booth as to the next sailing, and having confirmed that it was about 4:30pm, learnt that the terminal opening was due in about an hour. The lady behind the counter said that a Politician from Paris, the local Mayor, and dignitaries, plus Television, Press, and a jazz band were all attending. I walked off to the far end, ordered a coffee and a croissant, and sat where I could watch the fun, I had nowhere else to go.

As the time for the ceremony approached little knots of people began to assemble. Terminal security men stretched a ribbon, again in tricolour, across the concourse, thus dividing the building, and preventing anyone from passing. No-one took much notice, and those who wished to pass simply lifted the ribbon, stooped under it, and carried on. The effect of this was that the ribbon grew droopier and droopier and had to be re-tightened every few minutes. The band arrived and could be heard but not seen, tuning up, with snatches of "When the Saints go Marching In" and other jazz standards. Finally, when the massed crowd of at least fifty people could restrain themselves no longer, the official party arrived.

The men I assumed were the Politician and the Mayor each made typical Politicians speeches of about 15 minutes, which needed no translation, and would probably have generated the same interest if they had been speaking Outer Mongolian. It did ensure the dispersal of the crowd, who had clearly heard it all before. The T.V. crew took shots of the first few seconds of each speech and then roamed around taking pictures of the souls who were left. I may even have appeared on French T.V. I remember thinking that we might use

Politicians giving boring speeches for crowd control at home, when suddenly the band played an elaborate fanfare, a huge pair of scissors were produced, and to the music of the "Marseillaise" the ribbon was cut. Free drinks and little tit bits on trays appeared out of nowhere, the crowd re-appeared as if by a miracle to eat the freebees, while the jazz band let rip with their full repertoire.

I had seen enough, and now that I could pass unhindered up the concourse, I walked past the scrum which had developed round the food and drink, towards the doors and my bike. I was lucky that I hadn't been thrown out I suppose! I don't think I would have been very pleased to have a tramp attend any official opening of mine if I was a mayor. Just for a second or so, as I passed him, I thought he was going to give the nod to his minders, but when they saw I was heading for the door anyway, they simply watched me leave, then stationed one of their number to stop me coming back in.

I cycled towards the far end of the port, where I could see some bunting on the tops of masts flapping in the wind. I had just got close enough to see that it was an area of land alongside the dock, where boats had been pulled out for cleaning and repair, when the bike decided to come out in sympathy. You guessed it! The chain went again! I pushed it onto the boatyard and sat on the grass around its edge. I had to off load in order to turn the bike upside down and stand it on its saddle and handlebars. I was in no rush, the ferry was about 5hrs away, approaching from Poole. Having made the repairs, I was again in need of some facilities to wash up. I outlined earlier the lack of public toilets, and in my state, I decided that to approach a hotel would be tantamount to asking to be arrested. The terminal, was too far away, and to make matters worse, the thought of washing, was making me have certain other needs, which necessitated privacy. Help was at hand for about 100yards way there was a large grey/blue building with the words Fisherman's Union in French, which I translated as "There's bound to be a toilet and wash hand basin in there".

I approached the front door, abandoned the bike and my goods, because by now I was desperate, and scuttled inside. The place was clean but functional, and there was no one about. I scanned the foyer, no toilets. As I climbed each stair my need grew greater and my self-control less. I wasn't bothered about being in the building, I was certain that permission would be granted by anyone I met, given the circumstances. It was just that I didn't feel that I had the time to give a long explanation before nature cut short the conversation.

At last! There they were, on the 1st floor corridor. I don't wish to lower the tone, but I hope you will agree with me, that when you have controlled a desperate urge for a long time, it is at the moment that you are seconds away from "relief" that the need becomes almost too much to bear. It was at that moment a worker in the building, came out of the toilet, took one look at me, and said something which was an obvious challenge as to my trespassing. I had no time to bandy words with the gentleman, I resorted to the technique honed over days in the café at Bricquebec-en-Cotentin, shrugged my shoulders, gave him my long practised "Huh", and pushed past him towards salvation.

He said not a word. I can only presume that since it was the Union building, fishermen in the same disreputable state as me, visited the place on a regular basis. Equally, that they treated shore-based workers with the contempt, which I had expressed. Whatever the reason, he didn't argue, and I had no time to! Before he had time to change his mind both the cubicle and me were engaged.

Later, (sounds like something from the end of a chapter in a romance) I left the building, with a spring in my step, hands reasonably cleansed from grease and in a much happier frame of mind.

I found a small shop where I bought fruit juice, some cake, and a couple of apples, and spent the rest of my waiting time, back in the boatyard, alternately dozing and waking with a start, not wishing to miss a second boat. As boarding time grew near, I went back to the terminal and was pointedly ignored, if not totally isolated by everyone who passed by.

I suppose a shower was required, but my early start had prevented it. This together with my gruesome trainers (the only footwear I had) ensured that when we finally boarded, I had no trouble in finding an empty recliner.

Although the weather was fine, the crossing was terrible for me. I was returning, annoyed with myself, disappointed in that I had let down all my friends and relatives, and knowing that I had made a fool of myself. I had been away a week at most! I was most definitely going to take some stick! It was a good job that I had missed the first ferry, because if it had been the "Barfleur" and that crewman had carried on laughing, I don't think I would have seen the funny side this time.

I soon stopped feeling sorry for myself, and at about 10:30pm there, once more were the lights of Bournemouth, and soon we turned into Poole Harbour and were moored.

Despite all my misgivings, it felt good to be back home. It wasn't that I wanted my warm bed and a bath, or even regular food and drink. It was that the struggle to communicate was over. I could speak this language fluently. I had had a taste of the medicine we dish out to "Foreigners", and I had found it hard to take. To have to search for the right word all the time, to understand so little of what was being said, had left me feeling that I ought to have improved my French a long time ago. It had been a lot of fun, but it had really shown me my limitations too. I decided that I would try to improve.

However, speaking the language wasn't helping me get to the station, and I pushed the pedals round, arriving in time to board a "local", which was the last that night, and arrived at Bournemouth main station. There was no one on the platform except me after the local had gone, and the ticket office come porters' room was on the opposite side of the tracks. Hoping, rather than worrying, that someone might steal the blessed thing, I left the bike and my gear, and crossed over.

That smell again! I was kept at a distance while being told that I had missed the Birmingham train by several hours and that the next was at 06:45am. The window was about to close when I went into my tale of woe, which surprisingly enough, caused the night staff to allow me to remain on the station premises overnight. Admittedly I failed to make sufficient impression for them to let me sleep in the warm room where they were, and I ended up on the opposite platform on a bench, but stinkers can't be choosers. I rang home, to tell them I was back but delayed until the next day and settled down for the night.

If the station staff thought that a wooden bench would stop me sleeping, they couldn't have been more mistaken. Wrapped in my ex-army poncho, with my rolled-up tent as a pillow, that bench was positively stuffed with feathers compared with French soil. One or two goods trains came through the station during the night, and there were clanks and bangs, calls, and whistles, all of which registered somewhere in my mind, but it was a persistent shouting which roused me. It was 6:30am. It was very good of the night porter to give me my wake-up call, but where was my coffee and breakfast?

With the arrival of the train, I heaved the bike into the guard's van and, unsurprisingly, had little problem at that time of the morning, finding an empty seat, in an equally empty carriage. This remained the case even as the train gradually filled on its journey, what was their problem? I couldn't smell anything. Eventually as the train filled, passengers simply had to endure me to find a seat, but no-one, had the strength of character to actually sit by me. What it is not only to look like an onion seller but to smell like one as well.

I was Home! New Street Station was announced, and I was back where I had started only a week ago. Help was only a phone call away. My bike and its faithful friend the trailer were re-united, and within 30 minutes, I was outside the house. Was I met with tears and rejoicing? Was that the fatted calf I could hear bleating? No, it was the first of the laughs I was to hear over the next few weeks. Indeed, 10 years later, people still come up to me and say, in a voice tinged with disbelief "Are you the one who tried to cycle round France" then laugh as I confirm the truth of their assertion.

I was met by my loving wife, who tenderly and with great affection said, "You stink!!!" She denies this, but she made me strip, and wait in the garage, while she ran the bath. My clothes were picked up on a broom handle and shoved, into the washing machine. The trainers were transported by the same method to the dustbin. Only then was I allowed to pad naked through the house and up to the bathroom.

It is my opinion, that a soak in a hot bath comes close to being the best thing in the world. It's on a par with sinking into a soft mattress, covered with clean starchy sheets, having just eaten a large plate of bacon, eggs, baked beans, fried bread, mushrooms, topped by a dad sized mug of sweet tea, and then falling asleep for a day. When I woke up, I had some spectacular bruises, which had matured over the last few days. I viewed them in the bathroom mirror, and with some slight contortions could even see a portion of the ones I was carrying at the rear. Modesty prevented me from making a photographic record of them although I am sure they would have won prizes.

So, it ended! My first lone adventure into France on two wheels, and the last, for when a few weeks later I went back, I did so in the car. In the boot were airbeds which were inflatable via a pump attached to the battery, a light, powered by the same means, a sleeping bag, a mini stove with a fully stocked larder of goodies including baked beans. Changes of clothes this time, including, underwear and socks as well as casual wear, and sandals, shoes and of course, trainers.

This time when I got on the boat, there was no sign of the smart crew member. Pity because I was going to tell him that I had won "Le Tour!"

Well, I did win my own personal one! Despite all the laughs, and the jokes, all that mattered was that I hadn't given up. I was going back, and this time I knew I would have a superb holiday, travelling the length and breadth of the country. One day that may be another story.

Finis......

26th November 1966 - Paul and Jacqueline Weston

Proud Dad moment at the Passing Out day, Ryton Police
College, of Police Constable John Weston 1992.

Circa 1992 The family Weston, Dad – Paul, John,
Mom – Jackie, and Suzanne

First visit to Bricquebec-en-Cotentin. with Jackie 1993

First visit to Bricquebec-en-Cotentin, with Jackie 1993.

Dad excepting the Birmingham Mail Hero award from Jason
Donovan, 29 July 2008

Thanks to "Uncle" Bill and his trailer

Believed to be Mr and Mrs Begin's Farmhouse

Haf and Lew Owen, Jackie and Paul
Gothic Lodge Ladies Evening

Paul outside the house the morning of his adventure.

Mom and Dad First Trip to Australia, sometime after 2006, having had to learn to walk again, but being a hero

The campsite

Dad revisiting the tourist information
a little less exhausted than at first.

Dad with, Collette and Roger later in life.

Paul's bravery medal which he was awarded for preventing
an armed robbery in 2005

A "TOUR DE FRANCE"
Part 2

Chapter 11

I suffered after my return! And indeed, still have to defend my poor performance on regular occasions, when dining with friends, but only in a friendly and jocular way.

Nevertheless, I soon learnt that the easiest way to deflect the fact that I had only lasted a week was to lie. I think it was Herr Goebbels who said, "If you are going to lie make it a big one" on the basis that the more outrageous the lie, the easier it will be believed.

Mine was simply to say that the week's trip was always intended to be merely a preliminary assessment, prior to the real trip that was in the planning stage.

It was almost true, for as I said at the end of the story of the first solo journey, I did go back, but in the car, and my first attempt provided me with some places to re-visit at the start of my new foray into darkest France.

In the meantime, I had hung up the bicycle in the garage, where it still hangs gathering dust, while the tyres gradually deflate at about the same rate as my desire to ride the blessed thing again. From time to time, I look at it and think that I ought to get fit by taking it out for a spin. Then common-sense kicks in! I live on the top of a hill and no matter which way I go, I would have to climb a hill to return. If you add my experience with hills to my natural desire to stay in bed in the mornings, plus it being too dangerous to ride a bike at night, you can see why the dust is getting thicker and the tyres flatter.

It might make a good present for a grandchild one day, if only as an antique.

In hindsight, it was almost inevitable that I went back in the car. First because I had only used just over a week of my permitted "several" which the journey was supposed to have taken, and secondly because I still hadn't got the bug out of my system. I wanted to have at least a small adventure in my life!

The catalyst for my return plans strangely enough occurred at the funeral of a friend, Ken Woodford, when after the ceremony we were eating and drinking to his memory.

During a lull in the conversation, and these quiet moments do seem to occur at funerals. It doesn't matter whether the deceased was good and kind and a great loss, or even plain bad and never to be missed, but there comes a time when everyone runs out of nice things to say about him or her, and starts reaching for another sausage roll, sherry, or cup of tea. Well, it was during one of these "What shall we say next?" moments, when someone raised the subject of my abortive ride. I mentioned that this time, taking the advice of my wife, I was thinking of going back in the car, with all the advantages which that would bring when Ray Garrett, another friend in the group, passed comment that he knew a café owner in the small town of Evaillé, which was fairly close to Le Mans, and that if I were to pass that way, I was to be sure to pop in and pass his regards to these acquaintances. He described the lady and gentleman owners as very friendly, but shall we say, very plain of feature. That phrase particularly applied to the lady of the house, so in his opinion I would recognise them both without trouble. Besides, there were only two bars in the town!

I could hardly wait to get back home and pass on the glad tidings to my long-suffering wife. I now had another contact to add to my list, further decreasing my concerns about disaster. When a chain breaks on a bike it's a slight problem, when something goes wrong with a car in the middle of rural France it starts getting expensive, so having someone local made me feel a great deal better. I felt like General MacArthur, I would return.

Preparations began! The boot began to fill. My faithful igloo tent, boxes of food, the large size inflatable bed, sleeping bag, pillow, clothes, cooking equipment, and even courtesy of the car battery, electric light, and an electric pump to blow up the bed. The food box was my special favourite. Bacon, eggs, baked beans, cornflakes, Weetabix, sugar, coffee, dried milk, soups, biscuits, condensed milk, and all sorts of other tins of extras which just might come in handy. I declined to take the T.V. but remembered the can opener. Nothing was left to chance this time. The loading was under the personal supervision of Supreme Commander European operations, otherwise known as my wife, aka Jackie.

By the time everything was packed in tight, every space in my Vauxhall Carlton was needed, but experiencing a touch of déjà vu I drove away from my home, waving to the family, secure in the knowledge that I could now enjoy myself, the car would do the work.

After a steady drive to Poole, I couldn't help but notice, how easy everything seemed in comparison to my last visit. The roads seemed smooth, the signs easily visible, and no one seemed to take the slightest notice of me. To paraphrase a popular song, "What a difference a bike makes". The chippy near the ferry failed to recognise me, and it seemed a little boastful to say, "surely you remember me". I drove onto the ferry, parked the car, and went up to the passenger decks. It was the "Barfleur", just like my first trip, and I felt slightly disappointed that the laughing crewman was nowhere to be seen. We upped anchor, made the crossing, tied up in Cherbourg, and it all seemed so tame and unremarkable. Whereas before, everything I saw seemed part of the adventure, now the shine had gone. I remember hoping that things would improve. Perhaps having the car was making things too easy, did struggling to do something, sharpen the perception?

I had made up my mind that I would travel the same route I had travelled on the bike, and I noted the time as I drove off the ferry, it was 05:45am. The "wavers" were there but again I went unrecognised. They obviously only picked on lone cyclists prompted by my deckhand, who was probably even now, hiding behind a lifeboat, advising them by radio that some other poor fool like that fat "Anglais" from a few weeks ago was heading towards French soil.

My philosophical maundering about "struggle and perception" which might have done justice to a left-wing political organisation was quickly stopped by the dreaded hill out of the town. Never mind struggle; give me the slight pressure of my foot on the accelerator any day, as opposed to aching legs, a sore backside and sweat dripping everywhere.

Thus, I did pass the toilets, the little school, the old man's barn, and the shop where I left my hat, neglecting to erect the promised shrine to the patron saint of urinals, and failing to renew old friendships, principally because the speed of my journey was ensuring that everywhere was still closed.

I arrived in Bricquebec-en-Cotentin at 06:45am, completing in 60 minutes the journey that only a few weeks ago, had taken the whole day. I was still early! The square was deserted, the cafés shut, the information office silent. I decided to drive to the Begin's farm. It was as if I had just woken up on the morning of my leaving. Nothing was moving; it was just as I had left it. I drove into the farmyard. Stopped and walked into the camping field. I even made use of the toilet facilities, to give the Begins time to wake and offer me coffee, but to no avail. To think that I had believed his "I'm always up early". I decided that I would carry on driving south while the roads were empty and make some progress to my second stop.

Chapter 12

The sun came up as I drove down A and B roads, and although I was enjoying the relief of not having to push pedals around, there was definitely a sense of loss. Before, I could stop if I wanted to, and as you have read, I was stopped more than once going, now, I was almost back in the rat race I was trying to avoid. I caught a glimpse of something interesting but was past and gone. As for speaking to the local people that was clearly out of the question at the speed of a car.

At about 08:30am, on a nice piece of dual carriageway where there was a grass verge, I pulled in, and attacked the food stores. Those who know me well will confirm that I will eat almost anything, in any number of disgusting combinations, at any time of the day.

For instance,

Breakfast: sardines in their own oil spiced with hot chilli sauce on hot toast followed by Weetabix, coffee, and an apple.

Lunch: eggs, fried with a tin of baked beans added to the fatty residue, all mopped up with slices of bread.

Bedtime snack: a tin of creamed rice, spooned straight from the tin, after a cheese sandwich with sliced raw onion.

Any, or indeed all of these, are interchangeable, and of course, there are many other things in the cupboard, which are easily opened and disposed of prior to a genuine meal prepared by my wife.

It will therefore come as no surprise to learn that this particular morning's culinary delight, being in the country which prides itself on its food standards, was as follows:

A tin of sardines from the tin as a starter (because I couldn't wait for the cooked food I was doing), 2 eggs fried in butter (using my billycan and the little camping stove with the fuel pellets which looked like firelighters,) mixed in with a tin of baked beans, 2 slices of bread, and a banana all finished off with a mug of coffee made with 3 or 4 spoonful's of condensed milk and some McVities chocolate biscuits. After all that hard work, I was ready to find a village with a café, where I could re-introduce myself to a French breakfast.

I tidied up, dumped my litter in a convenient bin in a lay-by and drove off. It was now a lovely day. I just drove. I cannot say through which villages and towns I passed, which again, is a sad reflection on my mode of travel, but my general direction was towards Le Mans. Is there anyone who has not heard of Le Mans and the great 24 hrs race that passes round the town using normal roads as well as parts of the racetrack? What an atmosphere. I imagined the roar of the powerful touring cars, the famous names of the past. In front of me was the Mulsanne straight, where speeds in excess of 200mph are achieved. This was no dream; I was actually at the start of two and half miles of dead straight road. I was going to drive on a piece of history. My helmet was strapped on tightly, my goggles were down, the great engine purred under the bonnet waiting for feet hands and eyes all to co-ordinate into the man who is, was, and ever will be the greatest driver of all time, the flag dropped, I was off!

With ever increasing speed, man and machine thundered down the longest straight in the world, to find that "They" had built a traffic island halfway along it to slow everything down. The dream was shattered. How could they do it? Perhaps it was because so many everyday drivers like me, had tried to turn their dreams into reality with fatal results. Whatever the reason, I was disappointed as I opened the map and located the village of Evaillé, my designated camping spot.

If you arrive from the North, you drive down a slight hill, which is the main street of the village, towards the square and the church. I had noticed a small café on my right as I had driven down the hill and in the square was a second one. Since this one was apparently closed, and the decision having been made for me, I turned round and drove back up the hill to the first one I had noticed. The street was quite narrow, so I drove past, pulled half on the pavement and half off and locked up. As I walked towards the café, I noticed that it was virtually the only commercial premises in that section of the street and remembered the rest of the shops down in the square. I was soon to learn why the café was situated in its position. As I entered, every eye in the place turned towards me, every Adams apple paused in its motion, and there were quite a few people in there I can tell you. It was about 2:30pm and most of them looked like farmers, or manual workers of some sort. My son, when speaking of a particular town in Leicestershire, describes it as the same sort of place that you see in films about the Tennessee Hills. Where everyone plays the banjo, has no teeth, and sucks a pipe, and that's only the women. Well, this café was stocked with long lost relatives of the aforesaid folks. There was no doubting who was the owner. Apart from the fact that he was behind the counter, which tended to assist in identification, he was, as Ray Garrett described him a plain-featured man. I remember him as a grizzled chap with a big, droopy moustache, stained teeth, big nose, uncombed hair, and instantly recognisable as the man pictured to me back in England. My recollection may have been wrong, but he certainly did not look friendly in any way and the atmosphere in the bar had cooled in the few seconds since my arrival.

As I approached the counter, the owner's wife, for it could have been no other, and whose looks will live forever in my memory, appeared from some sort of a cooking area to the rear. Politeness prevents me from being specific, but "Plain in the extreme" does not do justice to her lack of beauty. Their marriage must have been pre-destined for they were indeed a matched pair, unique in the severity of their looks.

It was at this point that I made what was nearly a fatal mistake, discovering Weston's second law of travelling which is that. "Even a man with a very plain wife is capable of jealousy". Thinking I was being clever in identifying them both, and having been given both of their names, Guy, and Simone, I gallantly approached Madame. I would show these French, the way an Englishman could address a lady, I said something like "Good afternoon, you must be the beautiful Simone of whom I have heard so much" At least I think that was what I said? Her husband almost came over the bar at me! The bottle he was holding bounced on the bar just before his face turned bright red. From the gestures he was making, towards my throat, he was not at all impressed, that a total stranger had just walked into his bar and appeared to be on over familiar terms with his wife. He was shouting at me then at her, she was shouting at me then at him, I was backing towards the door, but the customers, scenting the possibility of an either "le crime passionnel" or at least a good argument to liven up the afternoon, had cut off my escape. I needed to explain and quickly. The accusations, the gestures, the sheer noise all were increasing, I said something about "un-Ami", a friend called "Ray Garrett", and as if I had waved a magic wand, it all stopped! "You know Ray?" "Yes" I answered, "I am from England on holiday, he said to say Hello". I couldn't believe it then, nor now, that this café owner could think so little of me and so much of his wife, that her fame as a lover could have spread as far as England, particularly since as far as I am aware she had never left the village. Similarly, that knowing just one other English person, could make such a difference to his attitude Vis a Vis another man and his wife. Still, it just goes to show you that love is blind, and in his case, he had the dog to go with the white cane.

Rays name had done the trick, however. The hubbub of talk from the customers subsided and I was asked how I knew Ray, who apparently at an earlier time had courted a young lady from the village who now lived in England? My explanation was accepted, and where minutes before my death at the hands of an insanely jealous husband looked highly likely, now, all was sweetness and light.

Food appeared, drinks were offered and with my faltering French causing enormous amusement, the events of my entering the premises were told and retold. At least, all the laughs, gestures, back slapping and nods at mine host and his wife, seemed to be pointed in my direction, so I assumed that was the cause of the merriment. I asked if anyone knew of a campsite nearby, since I had now been on the road and unwashed for about 24hrs and I needed a shower and to set up camp before night fell.

Further evidence of the transformation appeared. Whether it was because they were both embarrassed by the way they had reacted, or more likely given their extraordinary generosity to a complete stranger, the fact that despite their looks they were really nice gentle people, I was offered a shower. Simone ordered me across the road towards their house, (hence the reason for the closeness of the café and vice versa) and indicated that I should use their shower room and facilities. I found it hard to imagine such a turn of events back home, and their investing me with such trust. I stammered my thanks, went to the car, collected fresh underclothes, towels soap, razor etc and made for the front door. I looked back at the café window, and she indicated that I had the right place and shooed me in. The door was unlocked and walking through the passage, towards the kitchen, I saw the shower room that had been tacked on the side of the house. It was pretty basic but welcome. I stripped off, hung my clothes on a couple of pegs and began to shower. How long does a shower take, 3-4 minutes? Whatever the time interval on that day, thank God it was no longer than the time I took. They hadn't told me about Granny!

I had just finished dressing, which included the mandatory hopping on one leg in a confined space with only one half of your trousers on, when I heard a noise outside. I assumed it was Simone, and to give her a clue that I was still there, said in my best French accent "Alló". Instant mayhem ensued! The plastic curtain was pulled aside, and a large stick inserted, followed by a lady who by her looks must have been the mother of one or other of the M's but was so bad it could have been either. I could see her point of view. Was I a burglar?

A walk-in thief? What had I stolen or already done in the house? Was anything missing? I only hope she didn't entertain any thoughts of an assault on her virtue. Having escaped death at the hands of one branch of the family, I was about to experience it at the hands of another. I kept shouting "Café Café!" and pointing in the direction of the road, she, still brandishing the stick, prodded and poked me out of the house, screaming unintelligible French at the top of her voice. Holding my rolled-up towel that contained my washing gear in some sort of defensive position, I backed across the road at the mercy of the stick, while Granny, who had obviously fenced in the Olympics, thrust, and jabbed with painful skill. I was glad to open the door and seek the sanctuary of the bar. Little good did it do me, for she had now worked up a good head of steam, and still punctuating her tale with jabs at me, I heard the words "Gendarmerie". I couldn't believe it! When I got home last time, I experienced the relief of being able to communicate properly and here I was again, suffering from my inability to speak the language with fluency. The locals couldn't believe it either. I had only been in the Village 30 minutes and already had been accused of having had an affair with the licensee's wife and now was also strongly suspected of trying to violate a grandma!

"Vive Les Anglais"

They hadn't been entertained like this for years, and amongst the confusion they trooped up to the bar, ordered refills from Simone, who like them seemed to be enjoying the show. Guy was the one to whom most of the conversation was being addressed, so I assumed he was the son of the lady. I understood very little of the conversation, but at one point Granny seemed very insistent, and Guy equally positive that she was wrong, saying "Non-Non Non" several times. The customers were laughing. Having been thought of in terms of his wife, I was definitely being suggested as a candidate for his mother. Quietness began to descend as Granny began to listen to the explanation, but her anger transferred from me to her son. She was obviously berating him for letting me loose in the place without letting her know and began alternately shouting at him and turning to me making apologetic gestures. One of the regulars said something, and from the laughter, the general sense was that she was more upset that she hadn't been ravaged than if she had been. Everybody, including her, started laughing and I ended up being invited to a late afternoon meal and being offered a room over the café for the night. They wouldn't hear of me camping in view of the circumstances.

So, the rest of the afternoon passed. Me trying to explain about my family, my job, the holiday, and myself while all present listened patiently, and where one understood, translating to the rest what he thought I was trying to say. The last round of drinks being finished, and the novelty of my stupidity having worn off, Guy declared he was shut, the customers left, and the family members and I trooped over to the house for tea.

The meal was simple, comprising a terrine of rabbit, fresh bread, tomatoes and wine, but it was very tasty and reminded me of a similar meal my wife and I had eaten while visiting friends some years earlier, after which my wife was shown the beautiful white rabbits that had comprised the meal and felt heartily sick. I met another member of the family at tea, and I feel sure that if it had been her who had disturbed me in the shower, Guy would have taken a very different view of me. She was the very pretty (she could only have been adopted) 14-year-old daughter of the house, who thank God was either at school or otherwise occupied, while I was meeting Granny. I kept on thinking as we ate around that table, how extraordinary kind they were being to a complete stranger, who said he knew a friend of theirs. I suppose it was a return to the way we used to be in our villages, where doors were left open, and people were welcomed for what they were. I know I felt that we might be missing something at home, in comparison to these kind but volatile people.

I listened to what was being said, understood about a tenth of it, and was able to respond to about a quarter of that, but had no difficulty in understanding the side-to-side jiggle of the hand that has the universal meaning of "Would you like a drink?" I agreed I would and was presented with something I was told would be "Superb". The drink, which was absolutely clear, and was called "Gout", was in a small shot glass. Guy threw his back in one, and indicated I should follow suit. I did, and at first felt nothing. Then there was a deep warm sensation in my stomach followed by a taste in my mouth that I couldn't identify. I accepted another and as we downed them, he said something to his wife in which the word "Coffee" occurred and then took my arm and walked me through the kitchen, and out into the rear yard. By now the light was fading but he went towards two blue plastic barrels, which I at first took to be rainwater butts, and removed the lids that were covering them. I have never seen anything so disgusting in my life! They were both full of a festering mass of solids and liquid which were a mixture of colours, corresponding to whatever had been placed, fallen into, and drowned, or just plain rotted in them. The smell was appalling! The surface bubbled and slurped, and things came up on the bubbles, looked at the light, turned over and were carried back down into the mess, as it churned and pulsated with a life of its own. As I watched, he took of couple of loaves of bread which were obviously mouldy, some apples which were all brown and soft and the putrefying contents of a plastic bucket whose contents I had no desire to know, and carefully apportioned half into each barrel. The crust opened like something from a horror movie and swallowed the offering whole, causing a huge belch of gas to burst forth from one of them. Guy proudly said "Gout".

Apparently, in most villages, a licence is granted to someone to produce an alcoholic distillation from this rotting mess. Contributions from the villagers of anything that can rot and produce raw liquor are welcomed, and passed to the licence holder who allows the mess to ferment. When he judges it to be ready, he distils it, bottles it, and passes it back to the contributors. I had been privileged to witness the fermentation process. It was firm opinion that this new batch would be even better than the sample I had tried. Identify the taste! I didn't want to know what I had just drunk, and sincerely wished he hadn't shown me the stuff being made. All of this I picked up as I quickly drank two or three cups of coffee with plenty of sugar. While politely refusing any more of the local hooch. One more thing I learnt, was that the individual nature of the contents provided by each village, produced an equally individual taste. I was unable to confirm it, since with my lack of language skills, such a fine point would be difficult to make, but I wondered if the expression, "Chacun pour soi, gout" "each to his own" was derived from the local variations of this French firewater.

Accepting the invitation to return to the café for the evening session, I accompanied him back across the road, to find that the locals were already inside but they had observed the protocol of waiting for the licensee before they actually started drinking his stock. The rest of the time I spent in their company, passed in a blur, but I discovered Weston's third law of travelling, "Ones ability to speak a foreign language improves in direct proportion to the amount of alcohol one has consumed" I was fluent, or was it fluid, when I finally decided to make my way upstairs to one of the 6 or 7 rooms available. I was abandoned to my solitary sleep sometime during the course of the night/morning. I didn't hear a door close or word of goodbye and slept peacefully until the hens in the garden behind the café woke me. I washed and wandered around the place, which was a lot bigger than it looked from the bar alone, and again wondered what café owner in England would abandon a complete stranger in his property, with all his stock in the bar and cellars just waiting to be loaded into a car. Plain they might have been, but Simone and Guy certainly placed a lot of trust in people. I was treated to a continental breakfast and thanked both of them for their kindness several times. I asked for the cost of the nights lodging and was told firmly that there was no charge. It was only when I suggested that perhaps they would accept a gift for their daughter, that they grudgingly took some francs from me. They were lovely people!

They waved me off as I drove away towards my next destination, which was just south of Bressuire, which in turn was just south of Tours in the Loire valley. Here I planned to see if Lew and Haf Owen, some friends from England who owned a gîte near Bressuire were in residence, and then go onto the next village at Foret deux Sevres where there was a municipal campsite. The sun was up, the roads were clear, and I was back in the mood for adventure.

Chapter 13

The journey to Tours was uneventful. I stopped at a garage to fill up and to telephone home to report progress, both events being the high point of the day. I found the town very disappointing. Although the streets were wide dual carriageways with a large central divide, the buildings seemed to me to be uniformly grey and boring and the street layout rectangular. I was glad to get through it and out on the road to Saumur, following the road along the river.

This was more like it, everywhere there was room for a vine, and there was a vine. From the great Chateaux to the smallest cottage, it was clear that we were in a wine-producing region. Should anyone require further proof, as each specific growing area was reached, there were, like border posts between them, small buildings surrounding a courtyard, displaying signs advising passers-by that you could have a "Dégustation Libre - A free tasting" of the local vintage. Believe me, if I had stopped at every one of these that I saw, I would have been over the limit within 10 miles and paralytic after 20.

On arrival at Saumur, I went straight into the Office de

Tourism, which is on a crossroads near a bridge over the river and asked the whereabouts of a campsite. I was directed over the bridge and to the right, and in making the manoeuvre, recalled coming here with my wife a few years earlier. We had stayed overnight at a small Hotel called the "Hotel La Croix Verte – The Green Cross" and sure enough there it was on the left-hand side of the road. As we were leaving having had breakfast and paid the bill, the manager came running downstairs after us. He was carrying my suit that I had left in the wardrobe. He was saying something about it being too big for anybody to want to keep it. I made a right turn along the opposite bank of the river and at the end of the track saw the site. I found a spot, which suited, and parked up, on the hill overlooking the river by the chateau where the world famous "Cadre Noire De Saumur" train and ride their horses in display for the tourists. They can jump them completely off the ground, on the spot, and complete feats of horsemanship that I believe were used in times gone by on the field of battle, where the animals were used as part of the weaponry of the rider.

It was mid to late afternoon by now and the heat was stifling. Very few people were around and having pitched the tent, I decided I would have a paddle in the river, but had to abandon that idea, since it was almost bone dry, save for a brown looking stream right out in the middle of the sand and mud banks. Nothing was open! So, I did as the Romans were doing and had a little doze.

With the evening, the town awoke, and I had my choice of bistros, cafés, restaurants, bars, in which to eat, drink or just sit watching the world go by. In France, and indeed on the continent in general, there is no pressure to get you to buy, consume and get out to allow the next customer in. If you wish to, you may sit nursing one drink all night, and while I didn't do that, neither did I have so much that I would still be positive in the morning. I enjoyed myself, listening hard to the conversations around me, picking up 1 word in 10, and guessing the rest from the expressions and gestures. It's a skill you pick up quite quickly and one in which my wife is an expert, even though she can speak no languages at all. Time came for bed, and I walked back to the site, settled in and was soon blissfully unaware of anything. As dawn broke, I became aware of any number of different accents, all chattering as tents and campers were prepared for the next location along the river, and breakfasts were hastily thrown together and eaten on the run. I was in no rush (I hate getting up at any time, and especially in the morning) so I lay, waiting for all of them to go, so that I would have a bit of peace and quiet. When a relative silence had descended, I poked my head out of the flap and saw that it had been raining in the night. I dressed, brewed up some coffee, drank it and within 30 minutes was back on the road, having paid for the stay. Bressuire next stop.

Its only 20 or 30 miles to Bressuire at the very most so the journey was over pretty quickly. I found a Hôtel De La Gare opposite the railway yards on the corner of a small square and went in and ordered a toasted sandwich. I still can't get used to seeing men having a Continental breakfast of the "4 C's". A cigarette, a coffee, a cognac, and a cough! But this was only one of the many occasions when abroad, when I have seen it. The other essential requirement of being a "4 C's" man is to be sour faced, miserable and to growl when approached, with that back of the throat special French growl, which when a foreigner does it, sounds as if he is exaggerating. I watched as 3 or 4 "coughers" had an early morning conversation in the local "Growl" dialect, which in fairness I have to say the bartender seemed to understand. From time to time, he produced matches, coffees, and more drinks for his customers. They could have had a standing order I suppose but I think he genuinely understood the noises, backwards flicks of the head, and retching from the back of the nose, which preceded his filling the order. I couldn't stand it any longer, went back to the car and drove off out of the town towards La-Forêt-sur-Sévre, looking for the turnoff to the left which I knew would take me to where Lew and his wife Haf, owned the gîte.

I found it without any trouble, but no one was in so, I decided to continue to La-Forêt-sur-Sévre which was only 4 or 5 miles distant to find my site. The road as with most in France, was straight, and took me directly to my next scheduled campsite at La-Forêt-sur-Sévre. At the traffic island below the town, straight on will take you past a large pool almost like a village duck pond, fed by the stream that runs at the rear of the campsite. Go to the right and almost immediately the Municipal site is there on your left-hand side. It is a very spacious field, with, as I have said, a small stream across its far end, the main road on its left, and a caravan just inside the entrance on the right where the resident warden "Eric" lives, and alongside his caravan, the wash, shower, and laundry facilities. There were maybe 3 tents, a motor home and a couple of caravans in total on the field, and I chose a spot, directly opposite the entrance with my back to the stream. I backed the car in, to give easy access to the battery, and within 10 minutes had the tent up, and the pump inflating the bed. Having left Saumur without washing and shaving, I collected my gear and walked over to the shower block. My ablutions completed, I walked back out into the sunshine and met ERIC!!!

He looked more like a Norwegian or Dutch man than French, with striking blonde hair and muscular physique. His English was on a par with my French, and he told me the fees and confirmed my initial impressions as to where everything was. We chatted as well as we could and I explained that I would be back later, but that I was going to see if my friends were in. O.K. means O.K. in any language, and I went back over to the tent, laid sleeping bags and my other bits and pieces out. Zipped up the tent and drove away. Just as I reached the entrance, another camper van with 2 young women in it were arriving. Eric was standing by the driver's door smiling and pointing towards the town, while miming carrying a bag of shopping. I remember thinking, how helpful he was.

Still no sign of Lew and his wife, so I retraced my steps, and drove straight on at the island up the hill and made the right turn after 2 or 3 miles which took me to the farm owned by an ex-policeman called Roger, who had moved out here, married a French lady Collette and had now taken citizenship. He usually walked around wearing a T-shirt proclaiming in French that he was the mayor of the nearby village of Auxerre, and with the beret and small chin beard he looked it too. It wasn't my day; neither he nor his wife was in either, so I did what any self-respecting citizen would have done, found the local bar, went in, and ordered a coffee and cognac.

It was a typical town, one long main street, restaurants, cafés, butchers, bakers, etc. And as I sat there sipping away, I recalled Rogers and Collette's 5th Wedding Anniversary, which my wife and I had stumbled across some years earlier. The bride was re-dressed in her wedding gown, Roger like me had outgrown his wedding suit but was as nearly always in T-shirt and slacks, claiming a bad back made it impossible to get the suit on.

The bride's family were there from Paris, the tables were groaning with food and drink, everybody was kissing everyone else with that curious left right left gesture which is but isn't a kiss at all and we were made as welcome as if we had received an invitation. I thought of Maurice another ex-bobby and his wife, who lived next to Lew, and the rabbit terrine, and in such a haze of friendly memories, began to consider the possibility of buying an old house myself, and gradually doing it up.

It was about 7pm when I decided to revisit the gîte and this time, they were in. In the privacy of each other's company, Lew and his family only speak Welsh, and this facility with what to me is a second language, but to them is their natural one, has given them an edge when speaking French. At any rate, they seem to have no problem conversing with the neighbours. Of course, it could be that Lew has a capacity for drinking wine that is more than a match for the locals. Haf and Lew made me very welcome, and we sat and drank coffee in front of their home, as the late evening sun was just starting to lose its heat.

Across the road, were a couple of other houses, next door on the left a farm and on the right the smallholding and cottages that were owned by the aforesaid Maurice. They decided to take me down into the village where there was a café, which provided a "plat de Jour" meal of the day, for about a fiver. On arrival, the owner's wife had finished for the day but even so, was quite happy to provide us with a thick soup, chicken, vegetables, fresh bread and butter, and a fresh fruit salad, washed down with wine. The least I could do was to pay for what was, at a minute's notice, a simple but superb meal. I made my mind up that if this were a sample of the "meal of the day" then I would eat wherever I saw those words in similar places throughout the country.

Back at the gîte, more wine was consumed, and the effects began to show, as Lew and I, both members of choirs, sang duets to the stars, which with great patience none of the neighbours complained about. I even tried some of the local "Gout" which had been given to Lew, but which tasted exactly the same to me, although he assured me, I would notice the difference. I did, it was about 2am and the difference was that I had got to drive my car back to the campsite. I was offered a bed and sensibly accepted, sinking into the mattress, and falling asleep immediately.

When we meet, as we do quite often, being members of the same club here in England, I keep threatening to either hire their gîte or visit them again when they are there, to bring a further portion of Welsh/English culture to the French nation. To date, my wife prefers to visit the Greek Islands, or mainland Spain but as I write this, I feel the old urge to get back to that easy going lifestyle I found on my journey.

Back at the campsite, all was in order, more tents and caravans had arrived but there were still acres of room for everyone. I only stopped long enough to change clothes and then went off touring. Later that night on my return, the site was pleasantly but quietly active. Someone was strumming a guitar, and although I could hear children voices, they weren't doing battle, just being kids.

I woke to another sunny morning and setting up the little firelighter stove, began to cook bacon and eggs, and baked beans for my breakfast. The food was nearly ready, in the mess tin I was using, when I became aware of two little bare feet in front of me. They were attached to a little girl of about 6 who politely asked me "What are you doing?" I replied that I was going to have "petit dejeuner" "breakfast" at which she told me very seriously, that "they" had "café, du pain et de la confiture" not the rubbish I was eating, and "anyway what was it?" She recognised the "Oeufs", who wouldn't know an egg? But when I said that the strips of meat were "lard" "bacon" she declined to believe me. I understood her disbelief, for then, and still now, French bacon is almost like belly draft, and is used more for flavouring in stews, called "Cassoulet" rather than for eating on its own, since it is probably 95% fat. As for the baked beans, she knew that "Haricots" were white, and again I couldn't fault her. In all my time there, I never saw a tin of English style baked beans in any shop I entered. My breakfast was confirming to her how strange were "Les Anglais" She ran off towards the tent 60 yards or so to my left, but as I was raising my fork to my lips, returned with her little brother of about 4. He watched in amazement, as I ate, and she gave a running commentary on what it was I was eating. His name must have been Thomas, because as he sidled closer and looked longingly at my plate, it was clear he was only prepared to believe if he could taste. In awful French I told them they could try some of the food, but only if their parents said they could have some, and within seconds both had run off, shouting hysterically to their mom and then equally quickly, were back, sitting on the grass waiting for this culinary experience. I put some more smoky bacon in a fresh mess tin, cooked it and passed it to the customers. Very gingerly the little lad took a bite and swallowed as his sister watched. Even at her age she had reasoned that she would see if he died before trying her portion. She was almost too slow, because the boy, obviously enjoying the taste, had seen off his quota, and was reaching for hers when she realised that if she didn't hurry it would be gone. The remainder of the beans were dropped into the tin and sizzled as they warmed through. These disappeared just as quickly, as they discovered that cooked in the smoky bacon fat, and mopped up with some bread, beans might not be as healthy as coffee, jam, and bread, but they tasted twice as nice. The looks on their faces as the experienced a new taste sensation was priceless. With the honesty of all children, they wasted no time in long goodbyes now that the reason for their visit had been eaten, but shouted their thanks, and ran back to mom and dad. I could hear the torrent of excited gabbling that was coming from their tent, as they recounted their adventure to their parents. I had made at least 2 converts to cholesterol!

I stayed at the site for about a week and unsurprisingly used up all of my bacon supply in the first 3 days feeding my guests. I think that they would have been prepared to put up with just eating beans when the bacon ran out, I did have plenty in the stores, but they left the site before I did. On the day of their leaving, they both attended in front of the tent, with very solemn faces, and said in a lovely accent "Sank you very mooch". The little boy shook my hand, and the little girl kissed my cheek. I watched them drive away, waving to me out of the rear window of the 4-wheel drive, and thinking how sad! They might never eat smoky bacon and beans ever again.

It was the morning of the first day on the site. I was having a dream that I was back on Mr. Begins farm, sleeping on rough ground. It was so lifelike; I could have sworn I was actually, lying on the turf. I awoke, and I was! In the night, the inflatable bed had gone flat as a pancake. I had done my share of rough sleeping and was determined to get back to luxury, so I had my breakfast and then went to work. I checked the rubber plugs, which were all ok. I re-attached the electric pump and blew the bed up again. No good, somewhere there was a leak! After working my way around the bed, which was a double and just squeezed into the tent, I discovered that the leak was coming from the seam between the pillow and its main body. I had brought some patches, but this obviously needed some professional help. Eric directed me to a garage behind the main street of the village where for the umpteenth time, I met with that combination of Gallic co-operation and charm which makes me love the place, while occasionally hating it too.

The owner, was working on a Citroen and was deeply, and I have chosen that word specifically, involved in his work. Only his lower legs and feet were visible from beneath the bonnet, as he leant into the engine compartment of the vehicle. He was totally oblivious to my presence, which gave me the chance to cast a glance around the garage. I guessed that there was very little he couldn't do if asked by the local community. Apart from the obvious vehicular repairs, there was a plough in one corner, some fancy metalwork in another, welding and forging gear in another, and what I wanted, a tyre repair bay, on the other side of the car he was working on. Have you ever heard of that cartoon dog "Muttley" who does just that, mutters incomprehensible words under his breath, well this garage man was his human counterpart. "Huh hee huh, eeh uh eeh huh" went the conversation, in a French accent, which any self-respecting DIY mechanic trying to undo a rusted-on bolt knows translates as "Come on you ****".

I coughed gently, not wishing him to raise his head suddenly and smack it on the bonnet. He didn't do that, but I heard a classic French swearword "Merde", and he emerged sucking at a knuckle that was bleeding. Had our positions been reversed, I hate to think what attitude I might have showed to a foreign tourist, but this chap was great. I knew a word that approximated to "leak" and informed him that my bed had "Un petit crevaison" could he repair it? I told him where I was camping, and that Eric had sent me, at which he smiled broadly and said with a knowing smile "Aaaaah Eric". I knew I was missing something. My garage man by this time had over inflated the bed to really assess it and to get a better look at the area for repair.

Now in England, being the forthright and plain-speaking people we are, and not generally known for the use of poetic licence in daily speech, my man might have said "Its knackered mate". In La Forêt-sur-Sèvre, the owner turned slowly towards me, a look of great sadness on his face as he slowly released the trigger on the air line and holding the bed (which was slowly deflating as it lay across his greasy forearms) like a vet holding an injured hound, said with deep sincerity, "There is nothing I can do monsieur, it is dead!" With a black finger he indicated the seam I had found earlier. It was totally incapable of retaining air. The canvas had become porous over time, and he was right, it was dead! No one was ever going to repair it. I was hard pushed not to smile at his expressive use of the language, but it conveyed the meaning exactly. There was no way I was prepared to sleep on the ground again so at the worst contemplating sleeping in the car I asked "Did he know where I might buy another similar bed? Perhaps in Bressuire? Or Tours?" It was his considered opinion that Tours was the more likely since such an article might only be available in a specialist camping shop. I thanked him for his help and returned to the car, while he threw himself into the car's interior again, intent on getting that bolt undone. Any charge mate? "Non c'est libre." "No, it's free."

I had to drive through Bressuire to get to Tours so decided to check there first to save a possible journey. Do you remember the café where the professional French coughers were? Well just round the corner in a little street lined with conker trees, I saw a Police car and sure enough there was a Gendarmerie. I went in. Apart from the uniforms it could have been a pretty standard English County town station. There was Sergeant sitting at a desk, a Constable, typing something, and the usual assortment of posters on the walls. I checked these, and not finding myself wanted, introduced myself. I was taking my retirement, travelling through France camping, and learning the language. Did they know where I could replace my bed? There was the same considered silence, which I too have practised in the past on people at the counter, the same repetition of the request too "Replace the bed eh?" and then the grudging admission that this shop or that shop might sell such a thing. This was where routine really began. These two must have honed their skills over years. Working on tourists who could hardly speak the language. The Constable, as far as I could tell, disagreed with every potential supplier the Sergeant proposed, while he in turn argued as to the location of every bed seller and campsite provider the Constable put forward. I would love to have seen both or either of them, giving evidence in Court. I tried to back towards the door, but a large hand prevented me, "Non" they insisted, "They would find someone" After another 3 or 4 minutes of this comedy routine, I had an inspiration. "Nice Station" I said, "It's a bit like the one I used to work in England".

There was an immediate "Pardon?" "Yes" I said, "It's like my old station where I was in charge in Birmingham". Honesty compels me to tell you that my French might have been misinterpreted. I didn't think that I said that I was the Chief of Police for the City of Birmingham, but both stood up, and brushed themselves down and began to call me Sir. The Sergeant rattled off something to the Constable who disappeared out the back, while he came round the counter and invited me to sit. In passable English he asked me my rank, I recall Ron saying it was something like "Commissaire", so that's what I said, as I showed them my Retired Police Officers card. That confirmed my impression that I had been going about this the wrong way. I was offered coffee, asked where I was staying? Offered a meal, a tour of the station, free use of a car, why hadn't I told them I was coming? Could they help in any way? I took the coffee and after a few phone calls by the station staff, realised that Bressuire could not help. Tours was the place to go. I left the station, having thanked them both profusely and being saluted smartly as I drove away. I like to think that at least on that shift, tourists calling in to that station will receive help from a higher standard of service than the norm, on the basis of the fact that you never quite know whom you might be talking to!

Tours was a waste of time. I found two shops within a few streets of each other, without the need for the locals, both of which did not carry the type of bed I wanted. I drove back towards the camp, expecting a few poor night's sleep, while waiting for the next large town. As I turned into the site, there was a mass of activity in the centre of the field, with a large marquee being erected, complete with long folding tables, electric lights, and in the centre a large chest freezer. Good old Eric was supervising, so as soon as I had parked up, I walked across to find out what it was all about. It was a Boule's tournament, which for those who don't know is like bowls, except the bowls are made of metal and about as big as a cricket ball. A jack ball is thrown out on the ground and by lobbing the "boules" into the air and allowing them to roll on after hitting the ground, the one who gets closest wins. Of course, you can just lob them at the opponent's boule or even the jack, and spray metal everywhere. The competition was to start early next day and last through to the evening when the party would start. That was where the chest freezer came in. It was full of bottles of beer and wine. Eric and several of the organisers were checking that the contents of the freezer had travelled well, and I was invited to join. The wine was transported in what I can only describe as sterilised milk bottles, with crimped metal tops. This made it very easy to open on the edge of the chest.

My third law kicked in after the sharing of the 6th or 7th bottle of this local beverage, and I knew what the disciples felt like on Pentecost. Not only did I understand what was being said by everyone, but I was convinced that everyone knew what I was saying. We were all probably babbling at each other like idiots but with just a few "Hoh ee Hoh" I felt that I could convey the finest nuances of the language. One thing I did learn was what Eric did when he took ladies to the "Supermarket" and also why all the men looked knowingly at me when I used his name. I've heard it called some things in my time but "Let me show you the supermarket" isn't one of them. It was amazing; they really did seem to understand me! I was even invited to assist at the match as a visiting judge. A great honour, I was told. The testing of last week's vintage finished at about 1am in the morning, when it was decided that whoever woke first should get more wine since we seemed to have tested rather a lot. The last thing I remember, is Eric giving me a piece of foam rubber about single bed size, flat on one side, about 8 inches thick and a perfect replacement for my dead bed! Somebody must have understood what I was saying! I was a linguistic genius.

I awoke to music and the clash of metal against metal, and that was only my head! The competition had begun without the visiting judge. No one seemed to have noticed, and several teams were already deep in battle. The music came from a sound system, which had been installed, and the metal against metal was the boules of the combatants, who seemed more interested in destruction than winning. As I staggered towards the toilets and washrooms, a glass of last night's nectar was thrust into my hand by one of my fellow testers. It must have been a bad bottle, because in the morning it tasted like a parrot's cage, and that I assure you is a compliment. Refreshed, I had breakfast, and since no one seemed to need judging just yet, I drove out of the site to a roadside Wine seller I had noticed a few kilometres away. I don't know whether they are all the same, but this one was like a garage. It had huge stainless-steel vats of various types of wine. The level inside visible by a big glass tube on the outside. You could buy the stuff by the bottle, or jug, but the favoured method was to buy a large plastic container that was made in a sort of octagon shape. The beauty of this was that no matter which way up you put it, it was always on a flat side, so it didn't fall over. The manager took a sort of a petrol filler nozzle and away he went just like putting petrol in a car. I had taken a 25 litre one and bought the best wine they had. You can judge the quality for yourself, when I say that the container cost twice as much as the wine, and they should have given the container away.

Back at the site, several teams had been knocked out and had retired to the marquee, where the chest freezer was open. Miraculously, like the wedding at Cana, it seemed to refill with more wine as fast as it was emptied. Not only had we contributed to the replacement of last night's session, but every team had brought their own stock "Just in case". This was what I had come to see and be part of. Never mind the studied pouring of wine to glass, the swirl, and the nose inserted to savour the bouquet. Never mind the studiously chosen descriptions of "Strawberries, Oak and burnt lemon." These lads each had a bottle to themselves, which had the top knocked off quick sharp and lively and the contents taken in copious glugs, followed by a loud belch and a wipe of the hand across the mouth and or the drinker's moustache. Jilly and Oz eat your hearts out.

By this time the sun was up and with the drink flowing furiously, it was inevitable that a number of disputes would occur. There was a crackly roaring and tapping over the public address system, the decision of the visiting judge was required. I was just about to test a visiting bottle when my official talents were called for. I was surrounded by 4 or 5 gesticulating locals all of whom obviously thought I spoke their tongue, and shepherded towards one of the teams, where it seemed that murder was about to be done. With the invaluable Eric whispering in my ear, I learnt that someone had been jostled as the deciding boule was about to be thrown, and foul play was suspected. The jostler denied the offence, but the damage was done, the boule had been cast and had completely missed the designated area. Raising my hands for silence I asked the jostler if it had truly been an "error" and was assured, with much gesturing to heaven that it truly was. I looked at the man, then at the crowd, and was struck with the same disbelief that they were exhibiting in their faces. He was obviously lying. I then confirmed that the boules had all been missed. "Bien sur" it had dropped from his hand into the dust "Then" I declared, "the judgement was clear". The French were well known for their sportsmanship, if it had truly been an accident, and I was sure this man was truthful, then it was only sporting to let the thrower have another throw. Surely, they would not want it said that they were less sporting than the English." The jostler's side were glum, they could not now call their friend a liar, which he obviously was, while the other team were jubilant, and neither wanted to appear less than "Les Anglais." It was nip and tuck whether it was accepted, but perhaps the presence of the constable from Bressuire helped. I could see him at the back of the crowd nodding his head towards me, and gradually a consensus began to spread that the boule should be re-taken. A tense silence descended; the boule was cupped in the throwers hand, it swung back and forward, the feel for the distance being assessed and then it was delivered. It was an awful throw! It was nowhere near its target and meant that the jostler's team won. No one could argue with the judge however, the decision had been given fairly, and all seemed to agree that if he hadn't won with a second chance, the thrower probably wouldn't have won with the first either. Eric dragged me off back to the marquee with his arm round my shoulders, proudly taking credit for having selected, such a judge. If there were any more judgements needed, I never heard of them. On and on it went, food, drink, music, wine, noise, cheers, boos, laughter, cars starting, shouts, all whirling around like a fairground ride, and all the while my French improving to a standard I have never matched before or since. The championship was decided, and the winners declared and feted, though I never did find out who were the winning team. It didn't seem to matter much to anyone, for as they all began to drift away, and abandon the site to its regular customers, they all appeared to have had a great day.

The P.A. system was switched off, the lights except a bare bulb inside the marquee were all out and its sides were rolled up so that the site could be watched over as the last rites were performed. These consisted of Eric and several friends, who looked remarkably like the ones I had met the night before, including Monsieur Le Juge, finishing off anything still left within the freezer. There wasn't much and the within half an hour we were ready to leave when inspiration struck. They waited while I disappeared into the darkness to return in triumph, bearing my octagon, with a fresh 25litre supply. Despite the fact that it had been warmed in the sun in a plastic container for 8hrs, then allowed to cool during the evening, its vintage was declared to be "Superbe", the bouquet "Excellente", the temperature "Parfait". "Such a wine. I must have paid a fortune for it". There was really no need to waffle, I was glad to get rid of it and they would have drunk it no matter what it was like. Besides, it was the only wine available. Nevertheless, it was consumed with relish. Eric found some glasses in his caravan, and we sat around laughing at the world and each other, rising from the tables as individuals or in twos and threes to visit the toilets until it began to get light. I rose finally, wished them all "Good Night", and made my very weary way through the damp grass, towards my tent and the generously donated foam rubber. Some kind person switched off the sky and the noisy birds, and I was instantly asleep!

Had I lost a day? It felt as if I must have, for Eric was at the entrance offering his speciality tour to a new arrival and looking as fresh as a daisy, while I could cheerfully have gone back to sleep. It was in fact about 2pm, so I had had my 8hrs, but the idea of cooking breakfast did not appeal. I washed shaved and showered and decided to visit the town café for "plat du jour". It was last night all over again! As I walked in, all my friends were sat at a table drinking wine! Did they have special training or something? Were their livers removed at birth and two further kidneys attached instead? They pressed a drink on me; I refused and ordered lunch. They pressed a drink on me, I declined and ordered coffee. It arrived with a brandy. I gave in and drank both. It seemed rude not to return the gesture, so I raised my hand and gestured for a round. My friends joined me at the table, and I became an honorary member of café society, permitted to sit there all day doing nothing as long as someone was buying. I began to realise, that the compliments heaped upon my offering of the night before, might have been genuine, for the stuff we were now drinking was straight out of a bathtub. It was so acidic you could have sprinkled it on fish and chips. After 2 glasses, I made my excuses and left. Despite the honour of being accepted into their little group, I was way out of their league in terms of their capacity to drink, and I wanted it to stay that way.

In the course of the rest of the week, in which I stayed at the site, I found a large Son et Lumiére festival about 15 miles away. A restaurant called "The Windmills" for obvious reasons, and dozens of delightful villages and houses, each of which would have been a pleasure to stay in. It was the two men with their surveying equipment that made me decide to leave. "They weren't starting yet," said Eric. But the site was going to have a swimming pool next year, and when it closed for the season, the work would start. I decided that I would leave the next day, there was still plenty of France to see, and time was passing. Packing took very little time, and as I paid for the stay, and said my goodbyes to him, Eric told me to keep the sponge bed and we promised to meet again. He said he would say goodbye to the lads in the café for me. I don't like long farewells, and without a backward look I drove off up the hill out of the town, going south again towards another exciting adventure who knows where…….

Epilogue

I hope you enjoyed the story, every time I read it, I hear my dad's voice. He wrote this not long after he returned, but never finished it. Unfortunately, I only found out about it after his passing in August 2020 not from Covid like a huge amount of people of that time but from just being through too many things and that he was tired. I wish I'd have known about it before he'd gone, I would have encouraged him to write more as he had many adventures, particular this one:

Becoming a hero whilst trying to save a bank raid and taking a bullet in his femoral artery, 2 days after his first grandchild's birthday party and naming ceremony. Having a phone call that someone you love had been shot is something no one should have. Then the 4 months recuperation consisted of many heart attacks and sepsis, due to the huge wound through his leg and femoral artery, exiting behind his knee joint. One that in later life he used to tell the grandchildren (although they knew exactly what had happened) that he'd be bitten by a shark...... Having to learn to walk again and the journey that ensued over the next 15 years which 4 years before his death resulted in a stroke which took his ability to talk away from him, perhaps writing things down would have aided his recovery and reading the stories would have meant I could still hear his voice.

That would have been a good one....

Rest in Peace dad, forever in our thoughts, thanks for making us laugh with you one last time.

Monster xx (dad's pet name for me)

Milton Keynes UK
Ingram Content Group UK Ltd.
UKHW051133240624
444489UK00008B/66

9 781739 302078